MW00490642

LOVE YOUR
Body

LOVE YOUR *Body*

A Diet-Free Approach to Balanced Eating

BROOKE PARKER, R.D.

To my clients, who have allowed me to take them on the difficult yet precious road to recovery.

To my husband, who motivated me to start writing and then supported me the whole way through.

Walnut Springs Press, LLC
110 South 800 West
Brigham City, Utah 84302
http://walnutspringspress.blogspot.com

Copyright © 2009 by Brooke Parker

All rights reserved. This book, or parts thereof, may not be reproduced in any form without permission.
ISBN: 978-1-935217-37-4

Contents

Foreword

Over the past decade, I have seen Brooke Parker wear many hats, and she wears all of them with good humor and total commitment. She is a wonderful role model for incorporating nurturing and nourishment into all things food- and eating-related. I enjoyed Brooke as a creative, bright, and motivated student in the dietetics program at Utah State University, and I feel enormous pride in all that she has accomplished since then. She has provided nutrition education and counseling over the years in many settings to a wide variety of clients and patients. In many of those roles, Brooke has been a preceptor for my students completing practicum projects, so I've had abundant opportunities to experience the depth and breadth of her skills and compassion. Students enjoy Brooke's down-to-earth personality and sense of humor, and consistently report in their logs how much they learned from Brooke's counseling and teaching approaches. She relates extremely well to people, genuinely cares about them, and is gifted in her ability to tailor her efforts to each person. Brooke has such a "can-do" personality, and it rubs off on everyone she comes in contact with. When she speaks to groups, her passion and very direct (and sometimes disarmingly and charmingly blunt!) comments raise consciousness and awareness about these hard-to-talk-about issues, and her style is so totally approachable that her schedule is always full.

Brooke has made a difference in our community. She has made an impact on people struggling with the disordered eating issues she writes about in *Love Your Body*. I have confidently referred students to her for counseling, and I know that she helped them immensely. Local health-care providers who send patients to Brooke tell me that she is highly effective, realistic, and especially good with college-age clients (the population with the highest incidence of eating disorders). People get better with Brooke's help.

I am thrilled that Brooke has written this book and believe that *Love Your Body* will help many people struggling with their relationship with food. Brooke's clients and patients have made great strides towards recovery, and her readers will too. Her experience shows; the tools and guidance she includes offer a range of application and practice. Brooke's encouragement and willingness to open herself up and share her own struggles will provide readers with the confidence to take a leap—or a few small steps—in the direction of a healthier and more peaceful life.

Tamara Vitale, MS RD, Clinical Associate Professor
Department of Nutrition, Dietetics and Food Sciences
Utah State University

Introduction

Have you ever thought to yourself, on a sunny day when your house is clean, your work week is over, or your homework is done, that life would be wonderful if only you had a better body? If you're like most women, your thoughts might go something like this: "I am so fat! Look at all this flab! My stomach is huge. The cellulite on my thighs makes me want to throw up. I'm so ugly! Why can't I have more self-control and fix that disgusting part of my body? I'm weak. I'm gross. I'm worthless!" If these words seem harsh to you, then you probably haven't struggled with your own body image, and you are lucky. But if any of these phrases are all-too-familiar—if you really feel this way about your body—you're not alone.

I grew up in a loving LDS family. I liked myself, knew my family loved me, and had a grasp of my divine nature. I experienced having bad hair days, wishing I could look like the prettiest cheerleader, and feeling that my pants were too tight. I got over these feelings rather quickly, and back then I was generally at peace and content with myself. I ate what and when I wanted and thought nothing of it. I enjoyed activities because I really liked them, not because of the calories I could burn.

Then things changed. As I pursued a degree in nutrition, I learned to analyze and think a great deal about food. I got married, and with that came a lot of body-image issues. In addition, I began suffering from severe anxiety. Due to this combination of elements, my confidence, my relationships with others, and my spirituality took a nosedive. I became obsessed with feeling inadequate, fat, worthless, unlovable, and weak. I started to hate the amazing gift I had been blessed with—my healthy body. I could not enjoy life, progress as a person, or love my family. I was stuck in a place that scared me to death. With the help of a doctor, a therapist, my husband, and the Lord, I was able to avoid an eating disorder and come to find acceptance and peace once again.

After completing school, I began my career as a dietitian. A few years later, I started working with eating-disordered clients. I was apprehensive about taking on this challenging population, but I found that my life experiences had led me to these people. Since I had felt many of the same feelings, we could speak the same language. There was no need for them to hide anything or be embarrassed. I soon found myself fully invested in helping these girls regain their lives. As we talked, I could often feel the Holy Ghost directing my words. I learned that I was given certain challenges in my life in order to help other women overcome the same challenges. Eventually, I realized we were on a mission to fight Satan's plan to destroy women's precious souls.

Along these lines, while serving as Young Women general president, Susan W. Tanner declared:

> *He [Satan] has filled the world with lies and deceptions about the body. He tempts many to defile this great gift of the body through unchastity, immodesty, self-indulgence, and addictions. He seduces some to despise their bodies; others he tempts to worship their bodies. In either case, he entices the world to regard the body merely as an object. In the face of so many satanic falsehoods about the body, I want to raise my voice today in support of the sanctity of the body. I testify that the body is a gift to be treated with gratitude and respect.*

> *When we become other-oriented, or selfless, we develop an inner beauty of spirit that glows in our outward appearance. This is how we make ourselves in the Lord's image rather than the world's, and receive His image in our countenances.* (Susan W. Tanner, "The Sanctity of the Body," *Ensign,* Nov. 2005, 13)

The purpose of this life and our soul's journey through it should not be hampered by any kind of obsession with our bodies. Satan knows this and has created well-crafted media and worldly messages to keep women focused on their outward appearance.

By using tools in the areas of nutrition, body image, and anxiety, most of my clients were able to overcome the destructive pattern that had taken over their lives. My desire to share these techniques with a wider population inspired me to write this book.

My writing style in this book is often informal or conversational. I use this approach to create a relaxed, safe, understanding atmosphere, just as I do in my office. As you read this book, it might help you to imagine that you and I are sitting down talking together, one on one.

If you are searching for peace within your own body, this book is for you.

Section 1

FINDING A NEW
RELATIONSHIP WITH FOOD

Are you ready to explore a new realm of thinking when it comes to food? We are about to take a non-diet approach to healthy eating. As you probably know, the dieting mentality just does not work long term and can be exhausting.

In addition to slowing down your metabolism, dieting can lead to fear of high-calorie or high-carbohydrate foods, a mentality of being "good" or "bad" based on food choices, intensified urges to overeat, and even more unhappiness with your body and self-confidence.

No one bothers to mentions all of that on the cover a diet book! Instead, you are promised quick results if you follow a robotic diet plan full of *do*s and absolute *do not*s. While I can't guarantee results in a short amount of time or guarantee you will lose a certain amount of weight, my plan has NONE of the negative consequences of most popular diets. And I *can* guarantee you will find more peace with food, continue to eat all kinds of foods, learn how to listen to your body's signals, and customize your own balanced eating plan that will last you a lifetime.

Imagine yourself savoring all types of food without any guilt, making a choice based on what you *want*, not what you *should* have, and finally focusing on life, not food. If this sounds too good to be true, please just trust me and continue reading.

CHAPTER 1

Honoring Your Hunger and Fullness

The human body has an amazing system of checks and balances, with signals constantly channeled through the body to maintain order and harmony. As part of this system, a human being is born with the ability to identify hunger and fullness. This ensures that the baby takes in an adequate amount of energy—not too much and not too little. Infants respond very well to hunger cues—especially in the middle of the night—and more importantly, they can identify when they are full. (Have you ever tried to force a full baby to drink more milk?)

Unfortunately, society alters this balance as we age. We are offered food for comfort, to eliminate boredom, to socialize, to celebrate, to bond with family members, and the list goes on. It doesn't take long to lose touch with the signals the body tries to send us. Not long after a meal, my three-year-old son will often tell me that his stomach is starving for chocolate, because he sees someone else eat it. Clearly, he is responding to visual stimuli rather than physiological cues. On the other hand, one of my infant twins refuses to eat *anything* when she isn't hungry. I'm curious to see how long it will take for life to alter her sensitivity to hunger/fullness signals.

I've often related this process to a vehicle's fuel tank. A car can't run on an empty gas tank. On the other hand, pumping more fuel into a full tank only wastes gas and money. Wouldn't it be great if our bodies were that exact? Anorexic styles of eating would not work, and problems with obesity would diminish. Since our bodies do not work in such a precise way, we need a tool to help us reconnect with these crucial signals. The groundbreaking book *Intuitive Eating* includes a scale I find very useful.

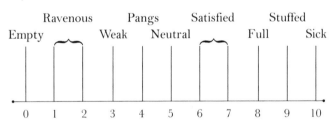

Evelyn Tribole and Elyse Resch, *Intuitive Eating: A Revolutionary Program that Works* (New York, St. Martin's Press, 2003), 72.

If you have spent time in a hospital or suffered from chronic pain, a medical professional may have asked you to rate your pain on a scale of 0 to 10. This rating style helps to put pain in a more accurate perspective. To simply say you're in a lot of pain—or in our case, hunger—does not mean much when a half hour later you give the same response. The trick with the hunger/fullness scale is to identify a feeling with each number so that you can honestly give an accurate assessment. Now let's go over each number.

0: EMPTY—A fasting state, going without food for 18 hours or more. When you drink a glass of water, you can feel it going into your stomach.

1–2: RAVENOUS—A state of hunger so intense you want to eat everything in the cupboard, whether you like the food or not.

3: WEAK—In this state, you may be physically weak, shaky, irritable, or unable to focus on mental tasks.

4: PANGS—Stomach starts to growl and you have the first thoughts of feeling hungry.

5: NEUTRAL—Body has enough energy to carry out daily tasks and gives no symptoms of hunger or discomfort.

6–7: SATISFIED—This is probably the most difficult place to identify. I like to describe it as a lack of any discomfort right after a meal, accompanied with the reassurance that you have enough energy to make it to the next meal or snack.

8: FULL—Slightly uncomfortable after a meal. I often give the scenario of not wanting to bend over for a while and possibly needing to undo the top button on your pants.

9: STUFFED—More discomfort than an 8. You may be reaching for an antacid. Often felt after leaving a favorite restaurant.

10: SICK—The pain is usually so bad that you need to lie down or even sleep it off. Unable to resume your normal routine for several hours. Often felt after a Thanksgiving feast or a binge.

You can probably identify with most or all of the symptoms in this rating system. Using this system can help you develop an eating pattern that optimizes your metabolism. Specifically, the goal is to begin eating at a 3 or 4 and stop at a 6 or 7. On paper, this makes sense and sounds quite simple, but most people have a hard time implementing it in real life.

Reaching This Balance

When the body reaches 0, 1, or even 2 on this scale, many factors are in place that can cause overeating. Emotionally, you may have felt deprived and find great comfort in eating for an extended period of time. In addition, according to Tribole and Resch, "Food deprivation or undereating drives neuropeptide Y (NPY) into action, causing the body to seek more carbohydrates" (ibid., 63–64). Typically, the emotional need and the chemical release are enough to lead to a binge style of eating. I tell my clients that if they let themselves reach a rating of 0, 1, or 2, they will overeat 99% of the time. *Deprivation doesn't work!*

Eating before your body gives any physical symptoms (rating 5 or above) is called emotional eating. This is probably the biggest obstacle our society faces in achieving a healthy energy balance. We can find a number of reasons to eat, and most have nothing to do with truly being hungry. The next section of this book will be devoted to handling this problem.

The body gives several signals when it needs food, and these are relatively easy to identify. On the other hand, the lack of symptoms is our goal at the end of eating—a much harder place to identify. Some tips for consistently reaching a 6 to 7 include:

- Take mini timeouts in your eating experience to internalize your feelings and actually have the chance to feel fullness.
- Stop eating when three-quarters of the food is gone, and ask yourself if you could make it to the next eating experience with enough energy to avoid ravenous symptoms.
- When the food does not taste as good as the first one or two bites did, the body is usually telling you it is full. This works especially well with rich foods such as cheesecake and milkshakes.

The most critical thing is to practice, practice, practice. It takes time to truly identify with this style of eating on a personal level. Your feelings and symptoms are unique to you alone.

Client Experiences

This style of eating is difficult for many to connect with at first. Every person I have worked with had room for improvement the next time we met. For those who go too long in between meals, this tool shows how deprivation often leads to ravenous eating. It is also an eye opener for the emotional eater who never truly gets hungry.

One particular client of mine who did well with this exercise was a bulimic who was getting tired of the binging and purging lifestyle. We only had a few weeks to work together before the university year ended and she went on summer break. I wasn't sure how to cram everything into two sessions, so I decided to start at the beginning and see how far we got. We reviewed the hunger/fullness chart, and I asked the client to chart her eating style for four days. Due to her busy schedule, we weren't able to meet for two weeks. I was excited when she came back a much calmer and more peaceful person. This simple exercise was enough to help her regulate her eating patterns. During the two weeks between our visits, she hadn't let herself feel ravenous, so the overwhelming need to binge was less intense. She wasn't afraid to honor her hunger anymore, because by doing so she diminished the out-of-control need to eat. That said, you don't have to have an eating disorder to benefit from this tool. We can all feel more balanced if we adhere to this principle.

Homework

Use the worksheet on the following page to chart your signals before and after meals. For each meal, record which number your hunger falls under before eating, and record your fullness 15 to 20 minutes after eating. Once you have completed the chart, look for patterns to see what you need to work on—emotional eating, timing of meals, etc.

Hunger/Fullness Chart

Day 1

Breakfast: _____ _____

Snack: _____ _____

Lunch: _____ _____

Snack: _____ _____

Dinner: _____ _____

Snack: _____ _____

Day 2

Breakfast: _____ _____

Snack: _____ _____

Lunch: _____ _____

Snack: _____ _____

Dinner: _____ _____

Snack: _____ _____

Hunger/Fullness Chart

Day 3

Breakfast: _____   _____

Snack: _____   _____

Lunch: _____   _____

Snack: _____   _____

Dinner: _____   _____

Snack: _____   _____

Day 4

Breakfast: _____   _____

Snack: _____   _____

Lunch: _____   _____

Snack: _____   _____

Dinner: _____   _____

Snack: _____   _____

CHAPTER 2

Emotional Eating

Emotional eating is a widespread problem, affecting all age groups, all social classes, and both genders. Every client of mine has had to deal with some form of emotional eating. As a reminder, emotional eating is eating anytime you are not physically hungry. In order to work on this concept, you must first learn to feel and recognize the hunger signals discussed in chapter 1. Whether you are trying to lose weight, stop binging, or just feel more balanced in your eating, this section will help.

So, why does a person choose to eat when she isn't hungry? It could be out of boredom (the most-common reason), stress, loneliness, or peer pressure. In early childhood, our parents give us food to console us, reward us, or just to keep us quiet. The habits we learn then carry on into adulthood and play a tremendous role in blocking the hunger/fullness signals. The deep-rooted emotions and habits surrounding this style of eating can lead to feelings of frustration, lack of control, and overanalyzing thoughts about food. It can also lead to a powerful deprivation cycle.

Picture the following scenario. I've just finished lunch at my favorite restaurant. I've listened to my fullness signals and even left some food on my plate. I feel good about myself and in balance with my body. I go back to a slow day at work, school, or home, and within 10 to 15 minutes I start to feel bored, stressed, and anxious. I know I'm not hungry but convince myself that just a little bit of my favorite snack food will make me feel better. So I grab a few Tootsie Rolls (my favorite treat in the office candy dish) to ease my discomfort. Unfortunately the elation doesn't last, and I'm back to the candy dish many more times. Now my food conscience kicks in to reprimand me: "How could you have blown such a good experience with lunch? Do you know how many calories you've just eaten? I can't believe you can't control yourself." In order to silence these thoughts, my willpower/disciplinarian voice then kicks in. "I am banned from all treats for the rest of the day and cannot eat again until dinner." Great, problem solved, or so I think. When the day is over and I get home, my stomach is definitely sending out all of the "3" hunger signals, but I can't eat yet because dinner is not for another hour. I also just went shopping and have a ton of delicious snack foods in the pantry. Now the mental battle over food begins. Finally, I can't handle the hunger pains or the restriction on all of the foods I love. I attack the pantry with vengeance until I'm full, and guess what? It's time for dinner. I've blown it yet again and must punish myself. The cycle is never-ending and very exhausting to both the body and the soul. And to think it all started with eating when I wasn't hungry! Although this scenario may be somewhat extreme, it has probably happened to you.

Next, we will talk about the components of emotional eating, and then use specific tools to overcome them. In most situations, we eat when we're not hungry to fill a void caused by loneliness, stress, boredom, or lack of stimulation. Have you ever noticed that when you are engaged in an activity you really enjoy—something that is mentally stimulating—you rarely if ever think about food or eating? On the other hand, have you ever written a long paper, had a job that required little mental or physical stimulation, or had nothing to do for a few hours? How many thoughts of food went through your head in the second scenario?

Restoring Activities

Bottom line, we often need more positive stimulation in our lives. Take care of yourself physically, emotionally, mentally, and spiritually, and then take a look at the diminished role emotional eating plays in your life. In order to fulfill your needs in so many of these areas, I recommend implementing a *daily* restoring activity. The following table lists things you can do to pamper yourself. I recommend that you implement at least one activity a day.

BODY	MIND	SPIRIT
sleeping	reading	meditation
resting	learning	prayer
relaxing	creating	singing
taking a bath	adventures	nature
stretching	time alone	art
haircut	yoga	music
back rub	gardening	dance
foot rub	being outdoors	laughing
facial	talking	family
sleeping in	cooking	poetry
hugs	journal writing	inspired reading
holding hands	dreaming	

Dialogue Questions

Let's dive into the dialogue you have with yourself before, during, and after eating for emotional reasons. The following questions will help walk you through such an experience.

1. Am I hungry, and if not, what am I feeling?
2. What do I need?
3. Are my thoughts positive and powerful?
4. What could I say to myself that would be positive and powerful?
5. What can I do instead of eating?

Let's use these questions to see if the earlier scenario could turn out a little better. As I leave my office to walk to the candy dish, I ask myself, "Am I hungry?" The honest answer is no. "What am I feeling?" This is where I have to analyze my emotions, and for many people this is new territory. It is often difficult to pinpoint a precise feeling, but you will get better at it over time. For this example, I'm going to list *boredom* as my emotion/feeling. "What do I need?" I need stimulation both for my body and my mind. "Are my thoughts positive and powerful?" They are definitely powerful but not so positive. It seems as if my body is screaming for sugar and the pleasant actions of chewing and swallowing. "This will make me feel so much better," I think. "I've got to have some right now." What could I say to myself that would be helpful? I might try something like, "A break from my boring tasks is what I really need. I will feel so much better in the long run if I choose a more productive way of handling my boredom right now. After I eat, the boredom will most likely still be there." So what can I do instead of eating? This is where creativity comes in. Perhaps I could go check my mail box, take a trip to the restroom, grab a drink of water, take a short walk outside, or run a message to a colleague. Obviously, this example is only one of thousands of situations you will face, but I hope you understand the process. Please use the worksheet on page 34 for help in dealing with your own personal situations.

Alternative Activities

On a talk show about making personal changes, the host commented that a habit is not broken; it is simply replaced by another behavior. Therefore, trying to eliminate emotional eating without substituting other activities for it usually doesn't work. The chart below gives some examples to try.

EMOTION/ SITUATION WHEN YOU ARE NOT HUNGRY	ACTIVITIES
BOREDOM	Exercise, sewing, crocheting, painting, crossword puzzles, computer games, scrapbooking, manicure or pedicure, call a friend, do simple house or yard tasks
STRESS	Listen to calming music, yoga, deep breathing, stretching, call a friend, read an inspirational book, exercise, enjoy nature
LONELINESS	Call a friend, exercise, start a fun project, e-mail, volunteer, write letters
DESIRE TO EAT WHEN WATCHING TV	Keep hands busy! Needlework, puzzles, crafts, scrapbooking
CELEBRATIONS/ SOCIAL GATHERINGS	Talk to others, carry around a glass of water, frequent the veggie tray, don't stand next to the food

Alternative Foods

Alternative foods are foods I recommend eating when you're not truly hungry but have a strong urge to eat that you cannot overcome. I normally tell my clients to try the 10-minute rule and then use this list of foods as a backup. Let me explain the 10-minute rule. When the desire to eat comes on strong and you know you're not hungry, look at the clock. Tell yourself you will do something on your alternative activities list for 10 minutes. If after that time you are still obsessing over food, go ahead and eat one of these foods. The list is composed of high volume/low-calorie foods, many of which are crunchy and therefore stimulate the brain and the oral sensory systems without adding a lot of energy. They are also foods that are easy to let go of.

- Light or fat-free popcorn
- Vegetables (raw or crunchy will stimulate the brain more)
- Salads with low-fat dressings
- Vegetable soups
- Ice water
- Gum
- Apples—especially sliced into small sections (your mind feels you are eating more)

Environment Tips

In a perfect world, the pampering, positive dialogue, alternate activities, and low-calorie foods would be enough. Unfortunately, our world is much too complex, so we need even more tricks up our sleeve. Changing your environment can help you succeed. The following may work for you.

Shopping

- Shop on a full stomach. Everything looks good when you're hungry.
- Shop from a list. Spontaneous purchases are usually the foods that get you in trouble.
- Buy foods that require preparation. Instead of the packaged cookies, buy the ingredients to make the cookies. This reduces spontaneous eating and puts more effort between you and the food.
- Buy more produce. It will come in handy for alternative foods.

Storing Food

- Keep high-risk foods out of sight. Remember, they are not forbidden; we are just trying to avoid frequent visual stimuli. Store these foods in the highest cupboard or in the back of the refrigerator or freezer. Never place a candy dish in your house, office, or anywhere else where you spend time. Place pans of baked goods on top of the refrigerator so that you aren't tempted to grab a bite every time you walk by.

- Store high-risk foods in opaque containers so you can't see them as easily.
- Keep low-risk, low-calorie foods available and in sight. I love to see fruit bowls sitting out and cut up veggies ready for eating.
- Don't keep food in your car, office, purse, or backpack unless it is a planned snack. Why set yourself up for a constant battle?
- Avoid eating from the food package. Studies have proven that we eat more when we eat straight from the package (see http://findarticles.com/p/articles/mi_m0813/is_2_31/ai_114325245/?tag=content;col1.). It's safer to remove a serving or snack-size portion of the food from the container and place it on a plate or in a bowl—and then put the food container away—before you begin eating.

Now that you are armed with all of these tips, remember to be realistic. No one is ever completely immune to emotional eating. You will fight it each day and will come up unsuccessful some of the time. As long as you are more aware and try to choose healthier alternatives most of the time, you will be in a better place with food and will start to feel at peace.

Client Experiences

One of my clients, a middle-aged woman, was very unhappy with life. She gave out much more than she received emotionally, mentally, and physically from her family, so she used food as a friend and as comfort. Food was always there for her; unfortunately, so were the guilt and the weight gain. When we discussed the concept of emotional eating, this client was amazed at how many of her needs were unfulfilled. She was not accustomed to thinking about or doing anything for herself. It took us weeks to get her to effectively use pampering activities, and it will take months or even years for her to learn to put herself first. Most people are surprised to learn that eating is not just about food.

When it comes to substituting an alternate activity for eating, many stories come to mind. One woman knitted an afghan during a stressful time of her life. Another ate so many carrots that her bathroom breaks came out bright orange. Other clients found new talents and hobbies such as painting, scrapbooking, and meditation. All were more balanced and happy after taking the steps to avoid emotional eating.

Emotional Eating Exercise

LIST 4 EMOTIONS OR SITUATIONS THAT MAY LEAD YOU TO EAT EVEN WHEN YOU ARE NOT HUNGRY	LIST ALTERNATIVE ACTIVITIES OR COPING STRATEGIES FOR EACH
1.	1.
2.	2.
3.	3.
4.	4.
ALTERNATIVE FOODS	

CHAPTER 3

Making Peace with Food

In this chapter, we will eliminate the line between "good" foods and "bad" foods. I want food to be just that to you—*food*, not an enemy or something to be so frightened of. Remember, a calorie is just a calorie, regardless of where is comes from.

Basically, "good" foods are those you can eat without guilt. "Bad" foods are those you have to restrict or punish yourself for eating. With my clients, typical "good" foods include things like fruits, vegetables, milk, yogurt, whole-wheat products, chicken, and fish. The "bad" list is usually longer and includes foods such as desserts, candy, ice cream, dressings, chips, pizza, cheese, beef, and white bread.

I had an interesting experience with this concept while presenting a lecture to a high school health class. In an effort to promote more balanced eating, I divided the chalkboard in half and asked the girls to call out their "good" and "bad" foods. Most of the girls' responses were typical. Then the boys took their turn, and I was surprised when they listed pizza, milkshakes, fries, cheeseburgers, and soda as their "good" foods. Asparagus, yogurt, spinach, and cantaloupe, came in as their bad foods. The overall difference? The boys choose foods based on taste, while the girls chose foods based on the amount of calories, fat, and carbohydrates they contained. In addition, the response from the girls when the boys listed their "good" foods was priceless. They couldn't even imagine having the freedom to eat so many savory, delicious foods without guilt. On the other hand, the boys couldn't believe the girls put so many restrictions and limitations on themselves. It was definitely a good insight into gender differences. The boys needed to use a little more thought in selecting healthy food choices, and the girls needed to relax and enjoy food more.

This experience made me ask some questions: At what age did this difference emerge? Why do girls become more focused on food and create so many restrictions and limitations that can only lead to guilt and poor feelings about themselves? In addition to influences such as peers and the media, what other factors lead to these negative perceptions about food? Whatever the answers, this is a serious issue.

Each girl I meet with can easily identify her "good" and "bad" foods. While this style of thinking is meant to promote healthy eating and control weight, it doesn't usually help with either objective. In fact, an individual who divides foods into "good" and "bad" categories usually feels a great deal of deprivation and guilt instead of balance. When I deem a food as "bad," what do I become if I eat that food? *Bad.* Therefore, I cannot allow myself to have something I really enjoy. I don't know about you, but I feel angry, hurt, irritable, and frustrated when someone tells me I can't have something I want. The amount of time I spend thinking about that particular food increases dramatically, and eventually I overindulge on what was taken away from me. In such situations, the outcome is usually the opposite of my intentions to be healthier—all because I went about it the wrong way.

Now we're going to embark on an exercise, developed by Tribole and Resch, that will put a brownie on the same playing field as an apple (ibid., 90–91). After all, each type of food has an important place in our lives. An apple can taste so refreshing. It is sweet, juicy, and crunchy all at the same time. A brownie is rich, smooth, and very filling. It also does things to my taste buds that nothing else can. So, how can I call a brownie bad and an apple good, when both taste great in different ways? This is where I will use one of my favorite lines again—*deprivation doesn't work*! It only comes back to haunt you. As soon as something that feels and tastes good is taken away, your cravings for that food skyrocket. Imagine choosing the food item that simply sounds the best at that particular moment. For example, you come in the house on a hot day after doing yard work. You're craving something juicy and cold to eat. You look in the refrigerator and see a big, red apple. It looks delicious and will hit the spot. You enjoy every bite. Later that same day, you attend a family birthday party where brownies are served. They smell and look amazing. You could turn them down and watch everyone else eat, then finally give in, eat too much, and feel guilty, or you could accept a brownie, enjoy every bite without guilt, and have a great time at the party. The second scenario is attainable, I promise! As Tribole and Resch declare, "The key to abolishing the pattern of restraint and subsequent overeating is to give yourself unconditional permission to eat" (ibid., 84).

In this exercise, you will choose your least scary "bad" food. Our objective is to make this forbidden, "bad" food less scary and overwhelming. The more exposure you have to a scary food, the less frightened you will become. You will learn to trust yourself to stop when you are full. This particular food will also become less tempting, since you now have permission to eat it whenever you want.

Client Experiences

I will never forget the first client I asked to try this exercise. We were both a little nervous. She chose potato chips as her forbidden food for the week. After the week was over, she shared her experience with me. At first, she'd eaten potato chips with almost every meal and snack, and she would sometimes eat half the bag. She couldn't believe I had given her access to this kind of food! After a few days, however, the novelty of eating unlimited amounts of potato chips started to wear off and she would only eat a large handful with each meal. The last two days of the experiment week, the client opted for other food choices at meals and chose not to eat potato chips, *not because she couldn't have them, but because she didn't want them.* She felt liberated from guilt and from the tempting power that potato chips had over her. We were both amazed and excited by the outcome, and we went on to tackle several more restricted foods in the same manner.

When I did this exercise myself, I chose Baby Ruth candy bars as my experiment food. I love the taste and texture of this candy bar and have a hard time controlling myself, so I was afraid to eat one. But that week, I gave myself access to the candy at every meal and snack. At first I chose a Baby Ruth as my breakfast with a glass of milk, and I included it in each snack and with all my meals. The first couple of days were like going to Disneyland, but then the excitement and adventure wore off. I started to want other foods instead and became satisfied with just one or two bites of a Baby Ruth at a time—and all because I could now have this treat anytime I wanted. It's so much easier to leave part of the candy bar (or any "bad" food) in the cupboard if you know you can have more later. If, on the other hand, you have only given in to a moment of weakness and know you will go right back to restricting, you will feel compelled to eat all of it right then and there.

Feel free to repeat this exercise as often as necessary, using a different food each time. Start with the least scary food and then proceed to the next least scary, and so on. Most of my clients internalized the lesson of this exercise after three or four foods, but don't worry if it takes you longer. Remember, the objective is to eliminate the idea of "bad" foods from your mind. I like to encourage my clients to think of it as most-of-the-time foods and some-of-the-time foods. Everything can fit into your diet comfortably if there is balance.

Making Peace with Food Exercise

1. Make a list of ALL the foods you love—anything that makes your mouth say, "Wow." To get started, try going through the food groups: breads and grains, fruits, vegetables, dairy, and meats. Then think about snack foods, dinner favorites, restaurant favorites, etc.
2. Place a check mark by foods you allow yourself to eat without restriction or judgment.
3. Circle foods you that restrict or feel guilty eating.
4. Now, this is where you'll need to trust me. Choose your least-scary circled food. For one week, give yourself unlimited access to this food whenever you're hungry. For example, if you choose peanut butter, you can have peanut butter on anything you want and for every meal if you want. The trick is to have this food readily available and then wait until you are hungry to eat it.

_____   _____

_____   _____

_____   _____

_____   _____

_____   _____

_____   _____

CHAPTER 4

Silencing the Food Police

Have you ever wanted to eat in silence? I'm not referring to an absence of external noise, but rather to a silence inside your mind. Since many internal voices compete for your attention while you eat, it may seem absurd to think that you can simply enjoy food. Imagine eating your favorite food and thinking of nothing except the taste, texture, and smell. It is possible!

In order to identify the internal voices that can affect your eating experiences, it is helpful to give each a name. Some voices may be your best friends; others, you may have never met. Once we go over these voices in detail, we will lay out a plan for controlling them.

The following is my take on the voices identified by the authors of *Intuitive Eating*. (See chart on pages 45–46.)

- FOOD POLICE—A cruel dictator voice that often demeans and restricts. Uses all-or-nothing phrases that can be quite ugly. These are thoughts you would never want to share with anyone. Often uses words like *can't, never, shouldn't, must, etc.* The Food Police says things like:

* The fat in that salad dressing will go right to your backside.
* You are not good enough to eat that piece of cake.
* What would everyone think if you ordered that?
* You are such a cow! I can't believe you ate so much.
* You blew it again. You are so weak.

- NUTRITION INFORMANT—Takes nutrition news, information, and trends way too far. Disguises the Food Police with supposed healthy intentions.
  * You can never eat butter, since it is loaded with saturated fat.
  * White bread is of the devil. Carbohydrates will make you gain so much weight.
  * If Oprah's trainer says to stop eating at 7:00 p.m, I have to stop at 5:00 p.m.

- DIET REBEL—An angry, frustrated child. Picture a two-year-old's greatest tantrum in the middle of a busy mall. This voice is easily hurt and lashes out to protect itself. Usually overcompensates when it finally has the floor. Is silenced once the Food Police and Nutrition Informant back off.
  * Sick of never eating what I want, so I'm going to eat a gallon of ice cream tonight.
  * Now that I'm alone, I can eat everything I want.
  * Hurry! Finish it before the Food Police pipe up.

- FOOD ANTHROPOLOGIST—a fact collector. Analyzes a situation without judging you.
  * You have a tendency to eat when bored between 3:00 p.m.—4:00 p.m.
  * Eating out with your sister-in-law causes your Food Police voices to speak out.
  * It's hard to guage fullness when you eat potato chips.
- NURTURER—someone who loves you unconditionally. For instance, I would use my husband or my mother's voice. The nurturer uses words such as *can, okay, may,* etc.
  * You can fit ALL foods into a healthy diet.
  * You are beautiful, strong, and able to handle hard situations.
  * So what if you overate. Next time you can come prepared with more tools.
- NUTRITION ALLY—helps you make healthy, moderate decisions.
  * You haven't had any fruit today. Have an apple first and then see if you're still hungry.
  * You could balance that rich entrée with a ton of steamed veggies and an ice water.
- REBEL ALLY—helps you stick up for yourself when feeling threatened.
  * "No, I really do not want any cake right now, thank you."
  * "I don't want to have any more conversations about dieting. There are other topics we could talk about."

Voice	Definition	How It Harms	How It Helps
FOOD POLICE	Inner judge and jury that determines if you are doing "good" or "bad."	Causes guilt and food worry. Full of judgment. Keeps you in the dieting world, and out of touch with hunger/fullness signals.	It doesn't.
NUTRITION INFORMANT	Provides nutrition evidence to keep you in line with dieting.	Uses nutrition as a vehicle to keep you dieting.	Once uncoupled with the Food Police, it becomes the Nutrition Ally and can help you make healthy choices without guilt.
DIET REBEL	Voice that bellows loudly in your head in opposition to what others tell you or you tell yourself.	Usually results in overeating, extreme restriction, or self-sabotage.	When the Diet Rebel becomes the Rebel Ally, it can help guard your food boundaries

Voice	Definition	How It Harms	How It Helps
FOOD ANTHRO-POLOGIST	A neutral observer that can give you a distant perspective into your eating world.	It doesn't.	Nonjudgmental. Keeps you in touch with your inner signals—biologically and psychologically.
NURTURER	Soft, gentle, soothing voice that reassures and never pressures.	It doesn't.	Helps to disarm the verbal assault from the Food Police. Gets you through the tough times.

(*Intuitive Eating*, 106)

Once you have a handle on the different styles of voices inside of your head, you can break them down and bring peace to your life. Bottom line—the Food Police thoughts have to be silenced and the Nurturer needs a ton of practice. The exercise on page 49 will help in identifying and re-scripting your harmful thoughts.

This exercise will try your patience and may be a bit difficult to complete, but please hang in there. I can't stress enough how important it is to identify these thoughts and deal with them. They are at the root of all your food/body image problems. The battle you are facing is probably not one someone else gave you, but a self-created battle of negative thoughts. It will take practice and time to become effective at turning a Food Police thought into a Nurturer thought, but it can be done.

You may find it helpful to review Chapter 8: "The Inner Dialogue," in conjunction with this chapter.

Client Experiences

I've found this exercise to be a good indication of a person's readiness to change. Those who only half-heartedly work on the assignments I give rarely complete this exercise. Those who do, learn a great deal about themselves and can change their lives. The bulimics I work with can truly identify with the Food Police and Diet Rebel, especially before and during a binge cycle. After a day of restrictions, the Diet Rebel always wins the battle and a binge/purge session occurs. The anorexics I work with live with harsh Food Police thoughts all day and find that their Diet Rebel lashes out at society, loved ones, and medical professionals by telling them not to eat. Either direction is harmful to the body and the soul.

Here are some nurturing thoughts my clients found helpful.

- "A calorie is just a calorie."
- "It's just food."
- "My life is so much more than food or these

thoughts."
- "I am capable of using my tools."
- "Deprivation *never* works."
- "Beauty comes in so many shapes and sizes."
- "*All* food fits into a balanced diet."
- "No big deal if I overate. I will listen to my body's signals and wait to eat again until I feel hungry."

Harmful Thoughts Dialogue Exercise

- Write down ALL Food Police/Nutrition Informant thoughts during a tough day/meal/snack.
- Leave a space after each thought.
- At a later time when you feel calm, go back and write in a Nurturer thought to counter each Food Police/Nutrition Informant thought. (You do not have to believe this thought.)
- I like to highlight my positive, nurturing thoughts and keep them handy. When I'm having a rough day or moment, I can pop them out and introduce logical, peaceful thoughts into my chaotic brain.

CHAPTER 5

The Satisfaction Factor

As Tribole and Resch advise, "If you feel truly satisfied with your eating experience, you will find that you eat less. . . . If you don't love it, don't eat it. If you love it, savor it" (ibid., 143). This is my favorite concept to teach—*enjoying* food again. Eating is meant to be pleasurable. Food is connected to almost every special occasion or holiday in our lives. Instead of dreading these occasions, let's start embracing them. Savor the taste, texture, aroma, and appearance of every food you eat. You will actually be able to move on much easier if you allow yourself to completely enjoy the food moment.

A common problem we have with the foods we love is that we eat them way too quickly. We may have been looking forward to a certain food for hours, days, or even weeks, but then we devour it in seconds. This leaves us wanting more because we didn't take the time to enjoy every aspect of the food. The fast-paced inhalation is often fueled by those annoying Food Police thoughts: "I shouldn't be eating this, so hurry before I have to make myself stop," or "Hurry before someone sees me eating this much." Let's take a new, nurturing approach to enjoy and then peacefully move away from the food. There are three steps to achieving this: (1) Become Aware, (2) Take Your Time, and (3) Check In and Then Move On.

Become Aware

The following tools will enable you to experience every aspect of your favorite foods.

- Ask yourself what you really want. Don't settle for something you feel you have to have, when all you want is a favorite food. Some examples: ordering a marinara dish when your favorite has Alfredo sauce, eating fat-free popcorn when you really want some ice cream, or eating a sandwich plain when a little mayo would hit the spot. In this situation , you will chase after that "phantom food" trying to fill the void with your "safe foods." Finally, you will probably end up eating the food you really wanted in the first place. Unfortunately, at that point you will no longer feel hungry because you have consumed numerous safer substitute foods along the way. Have you ever came home to find a plate of brownies a neighbor brought by and forbid yourself to have one even though you were hungry? You may have grabbed some rice cakes to compensate. They didn't hit the spot so you moved to the bag of baby carrots in your refrigerator. Still unsatisfied, you tried some crackers, then some grapes, and you finally gave in and ate a couple of the brownies. This hour-long process of "willpower" could have been eliminated by asking the simple question, "What do I really want right now?"

- Tune into your taste buds. Allow yourself to thoroughly enjoy the food. Focus on the following sensual qualities as listed in *Intuitive Eating:*
  * Taste
  * Texture
  * Aroma
  * Appearance
  * Temperature
  * Filling capacity (how long it takes to feel full) (ibid., 138–39)

In order to have a truly fulfilling experience with food, you need to experience everything it has to offer. *Take your time!* Ask questions and get in tune with your body. For example, a Twix candy bar is one of my favorites and was often my lunch during junior high. (Obviously, I knew nothing about nutrition then.) Until I started teaching this exercise, I have to admit I had never fully experienced all that a Twix has to offer. But as I paid attention and took my time, I felt the chocolate melting on one side of my mouth while the cookie started to break apart and dissolve on the other. Then the caramel slid down my tongue, sticking to my teeth and lingering in my mouth after I'd swallowed everything else. I enjoyed eating that Twix much more than I'd enjoyed eating any other Twix. I felt satisfied with just a couple of bites instead of needing to immediately devour the entire bar. This style of eating probably goes against your regular routine, but I guarantee that it is more rewarding and will help you to leave the food when you are full.

Please use the worksheet on page 57 to help work your way through three of your favorite foods.

Take Your Time

Most of us only eat slowly when we've been to the dentist and our mouth is numb. Our culture's fast pace has overflowed into our eating habits. We think things like, "How many tasks can I get done while eating lunch?" "I only have two minutes to eat dinner and run out the door," or "Great, another dining experience in the middle of traffic." How will we ever enjoy our food if we don't take the time to do so?

While you may like the concept of slower eating, it is much easier said than done. Here are just a few of the tips that have worked for my clients:

- Pay attention to how long it takes you to eat each meal. Make a goal to extend this time by 5 minutes. (Optimal: 20 to 30 minutes for a meal, 10 minutes for a snack.)
- Lay down your utensils between bites.

- Swallow each bite of food before taking the next.
- Take small bites.
- Drink more water during the meal or snack.
- Eat foods that require a lot of chewing, such as apples, popcorn, and raw vegetables.
- If possible, dine with others, and talk with them between bites of food.
- Pay attention to the taste and texture of each food.

Check In and Then Move On

To complete a healthy eating experience where you are aware and eat more slowly, it is vital to know when and how to stop. The following tips will help you assess your fullness and create pleasurable distractions you can move onto.

- Checking In: This is especially important for those who are afraid to allow themselves to enjoy food again. Many people think that once they start experiencing the joys of their favorite foods, they will never be able to stop. While I do want you to enjoy all foods again, I don't want you overeating all of those foods. Before you start eating a favorite food, decide on check-in times, such as when the food is halfway and then three-quarters gone. At these check-in points, ask yourself the following questions:
    * Does it still taste as good as the first one to two bites?
    * Am I starting to feel abdominal discomfort?
    * Will I be able to stay full until my next meal or snack?

* If I leave now, will I feel deprived or be satisfied?
• Moving On—This is our parachute in case the experience starts to take a nose dive. Before sitting down to a food you love and normally overeat, decide what to *do* or *eat* as soon as you rationally determine you are full. You need something to run to before the negative Food Police or the rebellious Diet Rebel voices can interfere.
* Activities
    - Go outside.
    - Throw the food away.
    - If eating out, put the food in a to-go box.
    - Make a phone call.
    - Run an errand.
    - Do a simple household chore.
    - Brush your teeth.
    - Play a musical instrument.
* Foods—Look for high volume/low calorie foods
    - Carrot sticks
    - Apple slices
    - Salad
    - Ice water
    - Gum

Client Example

A sweet girl I worked with was recovering from an eating disorder and was afraid to admit how much she loved the pies at Thanksgiving. In her mind, enjoyment would lead to an automatic binge. We both felt she was at a stage in her treatment where this would be a difficult but manageable exercise. I encouraged her to choose the pie that sounded and looked the best, and cut herself a normal-sized slice. She was then to make herself comfortable and take the time to enjoy each bite. Once she was halfway through the slice, she was to check in by determining if the pie still tasted as amazing as it did when she began. When the incredible taste started to diminish, my client was to automatically jump into a moving-on activity. Due to the strong hold the Food Police still had over her, we devised a fairly long list of options to choose from. She was scared to death to overeat. Some of our ideas included throwing the rest of the slice of pie away, offering to help with kitchen cleanup, going for a short walk outside, or chewing a piece of gum. This scenario took us a full session to plan and prepare for, and the client reported that the planning helped. She was still apprehensive to enjoy the food but because we had a plan, she wasn't terrified. She had a way out when or if the voices became too strong.

Clients without eating disorders have benefited from this experience as well. They started enjoying the foods that had controlled them and actually ate less at one sitting. Our motto: When you get all you need out of a food emotionally and mentally, it is so much easier to leave it. Those who inhale a food out of desperation, rebellion, or lack of time are always left wanting more, even if they are no longer physically hungry.

Experiencing More from Food

Choose three of your favorite foods to analyze. For each food, discover which elements you enjoy most. Let all of your senses be active in this exercise.

Food #1:
- Taste
- Texture
- Aroma
- Appearance
- Temperature
- Filling capacity

Food #2:
- Taste
- Texture
- Aroma
- Appearance
- Temperature
- Filling capacity

Food #3:
- Taste
- Texture
- Aroma
- Appearance
- Temperature
- Filling capacity

CHAPTER 6

Finding Your Own Healthy Balance

Now that we have a more intuitive approach to eating, we can talk about nutrition. That order may seem counterintuitive, but we had to get your perfectionistic thoughts out of the way before moving on. As you develop your long-term eating plan, it is important to individualize it to your needs and weaknesses. If you are an all-or-nothing personality, restricting sweets will only lead to heightened battles with the Food Police. If, on the other hand, you are nonchalant about what you eat, you may need more guidance and accountability in making healthier food choices. Here are a few systems that have worked for various types of people. Simply choose the one you relate to most, or create your own system.

Percentage Style

In the dietetic world we often talk about the 90/10 rule. If you follow this rule, 90% of the time you choose nutrient-dense foods, pay attention to body signals, and appropriately handle emotional eating challenges. The remaining 10% of the time you eat whatever you want, occasionally overeat at a social event, choose the richest dessert, or emotionally eat after a really rough day at work. Some people break up the percentages within a day, week, month, or even a year. This style allows you to underreact when living in the 10% and truly enjoy yourself. This style may work for some, but the longer I work with clients the more I see a need for an 80/20 lifestyle and possibly a 70/30 on weekends or special occasions. For me personally, the 90/10 rule puts way too much pressure on me and I worry constantly about messing up. This is where knowing yourself and your food tendencies will play a significant role. If you choose this system, be honest with yourself and find the ratio that gives you guidance without applying unneeded pressure.

"Most-of-the-time" and "Some-of-the-time"

This style works great for those who hate math and numbers. Each food is simply looked at as a "most-of-the-time" food or a "some-of-the-time" food. For example, a high-fiber cereal would be a "most-of-the-time" food due to its health benefits, while your favorite kid cereal would be a "some-of-the-time" choice to completely enjoy. This style of thinking is very relaxed but at the same time gives more nutrient-dense foods a higher priority.

Check-off System

This system works well for people who like to keep records. Specific foods or amounts are not listed because recording these details may lead to extreme overanalysis and obsessive food thoughts. All that is required is a simple check-off routine. With clients who struggle to eat anywhere near the recommended amounts of fruits, vegetables, calcium, or fiber, I have them place a sheet of paper on their refrigerator door. Every time they choose from a food group they are working on, they put a check mark on the chart. For example, if my goal is to consume three calcium-rich foods each day, I would place a check mark on my chart each time I ate milk, yogurt, or cheese. If I'm hungry for a snack and approach the fridge to find something to eat, I can see if I'm on track to reach my goal. If I have no check marks, I will be prompted to choose a glass of milk to drink instead of a soda or juice. This style keeps a well-intentioned person on track to consume more nutrient-dense foods.

Play around with each of these systems and find out which style best fits your personality. You may even find you like a combination of two or want to make up your own. The point is to keep everything in a peaceful, balanced perspective. Remember—*deprivation does not work!* It will come back to haunt you every time. Find something that encourages you without causing you stress. When you find the style that fits and incorporate it in your life, you will find a happier, healthier you.

Section 2

TACKLING ANXIETY

The word *tackling* appears in this title for a reason, and it's not just because I like football or because I frequently tell my son not to tackle his sisters. I use *tackling* because I actually want you to envision taking down an opponent.

It takes a great deal of strength and determination to defeat the thinking style called anxiety. *Anxiety* refers to an excess of negative or worrisome thoughts, usually about the future. Anxious thoughts can become so frequent and intense that a person begins to feel physical symptoms such as a pounding heart, rapid breathing, chest pain, excessive perspiration, and paranoia. Although you probably don't deal with anxiety on a serious level, everyone deals with some amount of anxiety. Most people are able to acknowledge the negative or worrisome thought, deal with or ignore it, and then move on. Some are not so fortunate and their lives become centered around their worry or fear.

If you were to ask a five-year-old girl if she wants to grow up to be a woman who hates her body, constantly feels like a failure, and is negative about everything in her life, she would probably laugh and wonder what's wrong with you. No one sets out to feel or think that way. No one wants a life full of doubt, negativity, and hopelessness. Ironically, it is often those happy, intelligent, driven, and well-loved little girls who end up dealing with the beast called anxiety. The desire for perfection, order, and acceptance can push a fragile soul too far if taken to the extreme. Soon, nothing is good enough and everything is seen as black and white, great or terrible, a success or a failure. Usually, it is at this point that I meet my clients for the first time. Their sweet souls are frail and damaged. They hate their so-called imperfections, focusing on them nearly all day long. This constant worry and self-doubt has left them feeling scared of everything, especially themselves and their thoughts. They would give anything to "run away" from their head for just a little while.

Women in our culture are especially vulnerable to anxiety as they try to live up to the ideals and expectations of a being a perfect mother, having a perfect body, building a perfect career, or experiencing a perfect marriage. Since this book focuses on body image and a balanced diet, most of the examples I give will be centered around those themes. I want women who constantly worry or feel guilty about food and their bodies to finally find peace of mind. As foreign as that idea may sound, it is possible.

The chapters in this section will outline concepts of

negative thinking and then provide positive alternatives. Each chapter includes a helpful worksheet. If you struggle to find and maintain an optimistic outlook, take the time to work through these next sections. It may be challenging at first, but if you stick with it, you will change your life.

CHAPTER 7

Simple Steps to Head Off Negativity

A small snowball on top of a snow-covered mountain may seem harmless, but what if someone comes along and gives the ball a little push? The snowball takes off slowly at first, but as it rolls, it gains momentum and size until it is a danger to anyone or anything in its path. So it is with thoughts. A couple of negative thoughts about your "failure" at dieting could be harmless by themselves. But what happens if you also shop for new jeans, step on the scale, receive an insensitive comment from a friend, eat a whole bag of potato chips, or find a plate of brownies at your door? Your one or two negative thoughts start to multiply quickly, and each subsequent thought is more personal and hurtful than the last. You may start to worry about the future and what others might think, or you might call yourself names and want to give up. Suddenly, your body begins to tense, your heart races, you start to cry, and you are scared and depressed. Your thoughts have become as harmful to you as the giant snowball could have been to anyone it hit.

As explained in the book *Attacking Anxiety & Depression,* taking the following steps will help you prevent these harmful, escalating feelings, and will allow you to get on with life and focus on the positive.

- Recognize that you are feeling anxious or negative.
    * Be honest with yourself in identifying which thoughts have the potential of becoming dangerous or escalating (multiplying quickly).
    * Learn to pick up on triggering situations or thoughts. Does being around a certain person bring on intense negative feelings? Do certain food situations make you very nervous? These situations will call for more awareness and preparation.
- Know that it is okay and normal to feel this way.
  Everyone has situations that make him or her feel vulnerable. Give yourself permission to be upset for a little while. Stressful situations are typical and are usually linked with some negative thinking. A problem only arises when the negative thoughts multiply and last for long periods of time. Chapter 8 will help you identify this "point of danger" and what you can do to avoid it.
- Breathe!
  You need to calm the body down. Rapid negative thoughts can actually send off chemical stimulants—such as adrenaline—in the body, which may lead to a racing heart, rapid breathing, sweating, tightness in the chest, or feelings of being crazy or out of control. Deep, slow

breathing is the easiest, most portable means to calm the body down. I recommend practicing this new technique while lying down. Place one hand just above your belly button and the other on your chest. The only part of your body that should move is your abdomen; your chest should remain still. Now comes the tricky part. Try to breathe in through your nose for two seconds. These seconds need to be the longest seconds of your life. You might want to say, "One thousand one, one thousand two" as slowly as you can. Then exhale through your mouth, this time counting for four seconds. At first, I always ran out of breath at about two and a half seconds, but after time and practice, this type of breathing became my safe place. Just slowing down and focusing on one thing can be so comforting.

- Talk positively to yourself.

  Help your brain relax or slow down by simply using positive thoughts, such as those listed below. A key point to remember is that you do not have to *believe* the thoughts. At first, you may feel uncomfortable telling yourself to think these thoughts. They might seem too cheesy, but trust me, they work. Statements followed by page numbers are taken from *Attacking Anxiety & Depression*.

  * "I have control of my thoughts."
  * "I can change my attitude."
  * "I am my own safe place." (1-3)
  * "I am worthy of inner peace."
  * "My best is good enough."

* "The more I practice positive thinking, the more comfortable it will become."
* "The real thing is never as bad as I imagine it to be."
* "What if everything turns out okay?"
* "It's not the worrisome thought that is the problem; it's the way I play it over and over in my head." (9-10)
* "No one is happy all of the time."
* "Treasure the precious present moment. Don't live in the past or worry about the future." (2-16)
* "If I don't like how I'm *feeling*, I need to change the way I'm *thinking*."
* "Deal, don't dwell." (8-8)
* "How can I underreact?" (6-8)

You'll be amazed how your body will respond to these calming, positive thoughts. Optimism may be foreign territory to many of us, but I hope you'll give this a try. The inner peace you will find is priceless.

- Distract, Distract, Distract!

When negative thoughts and worries refuse to go away even after you have gone through the previous steps, distraction is typically the only way out. Take some time to find out what you like to do. What makes you happy? What stimulates your brain or body in a good way? Who helps you think more positively? Where do you go to escape or relax? Diving into another area of life will often leave no time for you to dwell on negative worries. Some examples of distractions include:

* Going outside
* Walking, biking, running, or any other type of exercise
* Talking to a friend either in person or on the phone
* Watching or reading something humorous or inspiring
* Serving others
* Journal writing
* Puzzles of all kinds
* Scrapbooking or working on a craft

(See *Attacking Anxiety & Depression: A Self-Help, Self-Awareness Program for Stress, Anxiety, and Depression* [Oak Harbor, OH: Midwest Center for Stress and Anxiety, Inc., 2002], 2–5.)

Client Examples

When I ask clients to come up with distractions to use when they can't get rid of negative thoughts, their personalities truly emerge. Some of my clients knitted or painted, and one even loved to sit down with a new box of sharp crayons and a coloring book. One client escaped by watching baseball games, another loved to talk to her mother on the phone, and another loved watching chick flicks. When I'm most vulnerable, playing Free Cell on my computer is a great way to keep negative thoughts at bay. For you, I recommend anything that gets your full attention.

CHAPTER 8

The Inner Dialogue

Your inner dialogue is the conversation going on in your head when you are not speaking vocally. Often, there are many types of voices competing for your attention. These may include an optimist, a pessimist, a nurturer, an antagonist, a judge, a free spirit, a planner, and on and on. Our lives are affected by which voices we encourage and follow the most. If given the choice, most of us would choose to be an optimistic, nurturing, creative, on-the-ball person. Unfortunately, I've never met anyone who is all of those things all of the time. Everyone has ups and downs—sometimes significantly more downs than ups. During my extreme anxiety phase, I was all of the negative voices at least 90% of the day. At this point, I began to feel hopeless, trapped, and terrified. I can't tell you how many people told me to just relax, or to think positive, or that everything would be okay. I almost wanted to strangle those people, because at the time, relaxing and thinking positive thoughts were the hardest thing for me to do. I had become addicted to negative thinking much like an alcoholic becomes addicted to booze. I found some peace when I learned this style of thinking actually had a medical name: *anxiety*. (Throughout this chapter, I will interchangeably use *negative thinking* and *anxiety* in identifying this condition.) Just like the recovery of an alcoholic, it takes time and effort to overcome this style of thinking, but it is possible. The following topics and worksheets will walk you through the recovery process.

Abilities of a Non-Anxious Person

According to *Attacking Anxiety & Depression,* a non-anxious person possesses the ability to:

* Have compassion for self.
* Praise self and mean it.
* Talk to self in a relaxing, soothing way.
* Stop negative thoughts and quickly replace them with positive ones. (*Attacking Anxiety & Depression,* 3-2)

If the list above seems completely foreign to you, this section of the book has the potential to be life changing. If some of those concepts are occasionally difficult, this chapter might balance out your life in a rewarding way. The bottom line is that we need to be kind to ourselves and have a positive outlook. The judging has to stop. The looking for the worst outcome has to stop. The assuming what others think and internalizing those assumptions has to stop as well. We have to become comfortable with generating positive thoughts.

Negative Styles of Thinking

The main styles of negative thinking, as explained in *Attacking Anxiety & Depression,* are as follows:

1. *All or Nothing*—This is the black-and-white thinking many perfectionists struggle with. "The house is perfectly clean or it's a disaster." "I either get 100% on a test or I fail." "My body has to be the perfect size or I'm ugly." I think you get the point. There is no gray area, no room for human error, no room for you. This style of thinking sets you up to fail and then to punish yourself all day long.

2. *Negative Predictions or Jumping to Conclusions*—This classic "what-if" thinking will be discussed in detail in chapter 11. Basically, this style of thinking focuses on the worst-case scenario in any future event. Examples: "I will gain weight if I eat that." "I will fail if I try something new." "No one will talk to me at a party." This style of thinking is a complete waste of time, because you spend all of the present worrying about and becoming scared to death of a future that most likely does not exist. It's just not worth it.

3. *Filtering Information Negatively*—This style entails picking one negative detail to dwell on while disqualifying any positives. Examples: "My butt is too big, so I am completely ugly." "I struggle at math, so I am stupid." "I

have a head cold, so nothing on my vacation will be fun."
"These people are really fun to be around—NOT!"

4. *Mind-Reading or Assuming*—"They must be thinking."
    This style is all about putting thoughts in other people's
    minds and then living your life based on those thoughts.
    Examples: "I can't eat that much—he will think I am
    such a pig." "They must be talking about and making
    fun of me." "She must think I'm an idiot."

5. *Shoulds*—This style will be discussed in more detail in
    chapter 9. The *should*s are all of the expectations you set
    for yourself each day that are typically overexaggerated.
    Examples: "I should work out for three hours every day."
    "I should always have my hair and makeup done." "I
    should never eat that." (ibid., 3–10 to 3–11)

To overcome these negative thinking styles, we must first
acknowledge them, understand our motivation for doing
them, and then find an alternative. The following re-scripting
exercise will start you on the path to positive thinking. Like
anything worthwhile, you will need to put some work into it,
but the rewards will be greater than you can imagine.

First, pinpoint a situation or time when a lot of negative
thoughts are running through your head. If possible, write
them down as quickly as you can. If the situation is not suitable
for journaling, wait until you have time to jot them down. Try
to remember the exact wording.

Second, go through your list and try to counteract each

thought with a positive comeback. If you are still angry, frustrated, or anxious, you can wait a little while before thinking of positive comebacks. Remember that you don't have to *believe* the positive thought. You are only working on the ability to *form* a positive thought. (Many of mine sounded so cheesy to me at first.) Often, the easiest way to form a positive thought is to simply write down the exact opposite of the negative. Example: negative thought—"I will instantly gain weight if I eat that." Positive thought—"What if I don't gain weight by eating that and my body's metabolism takes care of everything?"

Third, grab a highlighter and mark all of the positive thoughts. When I'm consumed by negativity and can't come up with a positive thought internally, it's so easy to read what I've done before. Sometimes just a few moments of positive distraction can be enough to calm yourself down and put things in perspective.

The following examples may help you understand this process.

NEGATIVE THOUGHT—"I'm not good at relaxing."
POSITIVE COMEBACK—"I'm trying each day to get better."

NEGATIVE THOUGHT—"I wish I didn't get upset about being sad."
POSITIVE COMEBACK—"Everyone is sad sometimes."
NEGATIVE THOUGHT—"I will get fat if I eat bread."

POSITIVE COMEBACK—"I deserve to give my body fuel. I need carbs for brainpower."

NEGATIVE THOUGHT—"I feel uncomfortable when people see me eat."
POSITIVE COMEBACK—"Everyone has to eat. Most eating situations are not analyzed."

NEGATIVE THOUGHT—"Why can't I look like that person?"
POSITIVE COMEBACK—"I look good just the way I am. Her life is not perfect just because she is skinny."

Re-scripting Exercise

Negative Thought:

Positive Comeback:

Negative Thought:

Positive Comeback:

Negative Thought:

Positive Comeback:

Negative Thought:

Positive Comeback:

Negative Thought:

Positive Comeback:

CHAPTER 9

Creating Healthy Expectations

In this section, we will address the self-imposed rules or expectations you've created for yourself. *Attacking Anxiety & Depression* calls these rules *should*s and defines them as "expectations for yourself that you typically fall short of" (p. 4-4). The book's authors also explain that expectations are "usually unrealistic and not as important as you might think" (ibid.). In other words, *should*s typically set you up for constant failure.

Since you're reading this book, you probably have perfectionistic tendencies. Those who reach for perfection in many areas of their lives must eventually face the reality that they are human and therefore imperfect. For those who internalize these imperfections or failures, the repeated letdowns can be damaging to the soul. How much different would life be if you allowed for small slip ups, if you accepted your imperfections, and if you realized that life throws everyone unexpected curves? This concept can be divided into three categories: (1) Identifying Unhealthy Expectations, (2) What Is My Motivation? and (3) How Can I Fit into My Expectations Right Now?

Identifying Unhealthy Expectations

If you think you always fall short in many areas of your life—if you have a lot of *shoulds*—then you probably need to reword your expectations. With your expectations as they are, you will fail (at least in your own mind) every single day! How much confidence can you build in a life like that? To determine if you need to adjust your expectations, look for these key trigger words and phrases: *always, perfect, never, everyone, everything,* and *have to.* Read through these examples and see if you start to experience anxiety.

- "I should always be happy."
- "I should never eat sugary foods."
- "I must be liked by everyone."
- "I have to do everything perfectly."
- "I should always be in control."
- "I should have the perfect body."
- "I should be strong enough to withstand all 'bad' foods."
- "I should be thinner than everyone around me."

That life sounds completely depressing and terrible, doesn't it? Satan's trap is quite subtle. The desire for perfection is admirable, but when taken to the extreme it creates a life that is no longer about living but is about failing. These trigger words lead to black-and-white thinking. Something or someone is either good or bad, perfect or completely imperfect, happy or sad. There is nothing in the middle, no gray area. Where does that leave room for the imperfect human experience? Where is there room for growth or repentance or even the need for Jesus Christ, our Savior? Life is imperfect! We are imperfect! As soon as these two statements sink in, your life will become easier, gentler, and even happier.

Let's start by simply changing the words in our minds. Try replacing all of the trigger words discussed above, with more realistic words and phrases such as *sometimes, most of the time, get to, choose to, can be, try to,* and *do not.* Let's see how the statements listed above can change when we simply replace one or two words:

- "I can be happy most of the time."
- "I get to eat sugary foods some of the time."
- "I do not have to be liked by everyone."
- "I can have a healthy, beautiful body."
- "I do not have to be in control all of the time."
- "There are no 'bad' foods, just 'some-of-the-time' and 'most-of-the-time' foods."

Do you breathe a little easier when you read the second list of statements? You should. They allow for the human experience. They allow for choice, flexibility, and even improvement.

When I ask my clients to change their expectations, the most common fear they express is the fear of giving up. If they change their expectations to allow for leniency, they feel they are giving up on all of their goals. Even worse, they imagine all of their worst nightmares coming true. If they give up the rule of never eating sweets, they imagine themselves *only* eating sweets and not being able to stop. Because the mind of a perfectionist tends to conjure up the worst possible alternative, these clients believe that giving up on the perfect body will automatically lead to an ugly, obese body. My job is to help them—and you—see all of the positives that can come from more realistic expectations. The most important benefit of a change in expectations is the daily release of tension and failure. You can have more patience with yourself and even feel more love and acceptance toward yourself, all from changing a few simple words. The exercise at the end of this chapter will walk you through this process.

What Is My Motivation?

Very few people ever analyze this part of their expectations. Ask yourself, "Why do I need to reach this extreme in my life?" I use the word *extreme* because if we often fall short of a goal, it is usually because it is set too high or is unrealistic. In order to get you thinking about your motivation, please use the questions below for each of your previously listed expectations.

- Would I ask this of anyone else?
- Am I overreacting out of fear?
- Am I trying to be perfect?
- Whom am I trying to impress?
- Do I really have to control this?
- Am I trying to compete against others?
- Is this *my* goal or is it my parents', spouse's, etc.?

Let's go through each of these questions to bring home some important points.

WOULD I ASK THIS OF ANYONE ELSE?

Would you ask your daughter, sister, mother, or best friend to stop at nothing to have the perfect body? Would you ask them to never eat "bad" foods? Would you expect them to be completely dissatisfied with what they are now? The answer I always receive to these questions is a resounding *no!* The first step in re-writing expectations is to learn to be loving and gentle with yourself.

AM I OVERREACTING OUT OF FEAR?

This question usually helps with the expectation of never eating certain foods. If you're afraid you'll eat too much of a certain food, completely denying yourself of it might seem to be the safest option. The mindset is that by eliminating any exposure to the food, you avoid any scary situations with it. The problem with this style of thinking is that it's extreme or black-or-white in nature. What happens if your children make your favorite cake for your birthday and you have an expectation of no sweets, no exceptions. Do you break their hearts over something so extreme? If you find many of your expectations have been made because of fear, the tools in Section 1 will empower you. The more prepared you are for scary situations, the less you need to fear.

AM I TRYING TO BE PERFECT?

If you are hung up on the perfect body or the perfect diet, you most likely negate anything that is good or positive. If one part of your body is not perfect, does that instantly disqualify any beautiful assets you may have? According to extreme expectations, it does just that. But I want you to start accepting and acknowledging more often those areas of your body that are beautiful and perfect. Ask yourself: "What are my favorite parts of my body? What healthy aspects do I consistently have in my diet?" Acknowledging your successes and assets allows you to realize that perfection is not the only way to be good or be happy.

WHOM AM I TRYING TO IMPRESS?

Am I trying to gain someone's approval? If I can't be accepted and loved for who I am, do I really want to be around this person? Take a look inside yourself and think about what really matters. Find ways to enhance your personality and your favorite parts of your body.

Do I really have to control this?

In many cases, you might need to humble yourself and realize that you *do not* need to control everything. This life is about relying on a Higher Power for help when it seems you can't control anything.

Am I trying to compete against others?

If you find your identity wrapped up in your appearance or body size, you should focus on this question. Trying to be the thinnest, the prettiest, or the most popular will only lead you down a path of unhappiness. In fact, constant comparisons tend to fill a person with anxious, negative feelings. Start to acknowledge and support others in their assets, instead of using them to belittle yourself. So what if your best friend has smaller thighs than you? You may have a better complexion. We all have things we love about ourselves and things we could do without. Seek for the traits that really matter, such as honesty, listening abilities, charity, generosity, and intelligence.

Is this MY goal?

If your parents, spouse, or friends are pushing unrealistic goals on you, learn to stick up for yourself. Learn to be more assertive. If others base their love for you on your body size or your eating habits, they have their own issues and you would do well to limit the time you spend with them.

How Can I Fit into My Expectations Right Now?

Now that we've identified unhealthy wording and motives behind our expectations, let's figure out the proper way to create healthy expectations for ourselves. Please remember that changing an expectation does not mean you are giving up. It is simply a better way of achieving your goal, a method that focuses on progress instead of failure.

First, you'll need to assess which expectations need to be thrown out. Those things you cannot control or those expectations imposed by others should be the first to go. Second, you'll need to identify a flexible range you are comfortable with, and most importantly, that you fit into right now. For example, if Suzanne has an expectation of only one dessert per week but finds she typically has at least two per day, her expectation is obviously unrealistic and sets her up for failure each day. A more appropriate, flexible expectation would be to have one to two treats per day. (I recommend using a range with each expectation to allow for life's inconsistencies.) Now Suzanne can live without the deprivation feelings stirred up from an unrealistic expectation. She also has the room to choose, from a moderate range, which number of desserts will fit best in her day. She has room for progress but the key is that *she fits into her expectation right now.* She is no longer failing each day.

Another example: Lindsey is very unhappy with her pant size. Her current expectation is to fit into her "skinny jeans" from two years ago. Each time she tries them on, she is reminded what a "failure" she is and feels an urgency to lose weight as quickly as she can and at nearly any cost. If she were to adjust her expectations, she would find that gradual progress towards a goal will help her achieve more. I would recommend that Lindsey find jeans that fit her body *now* and help her feel attractive *now*. She could then put the focus on becoming stronger and more fit. She could create expectations or a goal of exercising two to four days a week with an emphasis of becoming stronger and gaining more endurance every two weeks. She could also set an expectation or goal of increasing her intake of fruits and vegetables to three to four servings per day. Once she does this, Lindsey feels she is successful—on a daily basis—in making progress at things she can control. The "skinny jeans" expectation looked too far into the future and seemed overwhelming, causing her to feel hopeless and to put less effort into increased activity and better eating habits. She instead chose to focus on the things she could work on *today* and how to accept and love *today*'s body.

I can't stress enough the power of fitting into each of your expectations now. When you do, time pressures will diminish, your self-respect will increase, and you will come much closer to meeting your goals. I can't promise that Suzanne will have no more dessert issues or that Lindsey will fit into her "skinny jeans," but I can promise that both women will be happier, healthier, and progressing toward a more balanced life.

I encourage you to go through the "Expectations"

worksheet on page 86. Cross out or eliminate those expectations that just aren't worth it anymore. Reword those that use harsh, negative words. Finally, find a way to fit into your expectation now by creating a range to work toward. Good luck!

Creating Healthy Expectations Exercise

List the top five expectations you typically fall short of (look for the negative absolute words—*never, always, must, perfect,* etc.):

1.

2.

3.

4.

5.

Reworded expectations:

1.

2.

3.

4.

5.

CHAPTER 10

Put An End to Worry

Envision in your mind a wheel. We'll call it the "worry wheel." Now let's start slowly tacking a few simple concerns onto the worry wheel. These few worries bring to mind other concerns, so add those too. Soon, you realize that the more worries you pile on the wheel, the more momentum it gains. After a while you can't seem to make it stop and may even start throwing any worry you've ever thought about on it. You might start out with a simple worry such as, "What am I going to make for dinner?" Then you start to worry how you look too terrible to go to the grocery store, how groceries are so expensive right now, how you want to get takeout food but that will completely ruin your diet, and how you feel so out of control, big, and ugly. Wow, all that came from trying to decide what to make for dinner! This circular way of thinking becomes almost second nature if practiced long enough, and sometimes we "practice" it without even realizing it.

Worrying can be such an exhausting habit. The present

moment is bombarded with concerns about the past and/or the future. Those who become "professional worriers" can start to feel protected by their worries. My clients often state, "If I somehow worry about them long enough and hard enough, I can fix my problems." There is one main flaw with this style of thinking: Worries are thoughts, not actions. Worrying doesn't get things done, so it doesn't help! I like to relate worry to a frequent scene in the cartoon *The Flintstones*. Fred and Barney are always driving around in a little car that looks like a golf cart. Have you ever noticed that the contraption always needs a jump-start of fast-flying feet and crazy sound effects to begin moving? It is that moment of extreme effort on the part of the Flintstones and the Rubbles that I compare to worry. They are working so hard but getting nowhere! Worry takes a great deal of brain power and almost always gets you nowhere.

Now that we've reminded ourselves how ineffective it is to worry, I want you to try a simple exercise to put things in perspective. Find a time during the day to write down your worries. Sometimes, it is beneficial to have a designated 'worry time' to enable you to put the little worries throughout the day on the back burner of your mind. Simply tell yourself, "I can't focus on that worry right now, since it is not my "worry time." The best thing about this exercise is that many worries are simply forgotten about when "worry time" comes around. Other people find it beneficial to do this exercise when they are feeling overwhelmed by worries, no matter what time of day it is. You may want to try both methods to see which matches your personality and lifestyle the best.

Here is an example to show how this can work. (To personalize this exercise, use the worksheet on page 94 to categorize your worries.)

1. List of possible worries at 10:30 p.m.

House is a mess	Kids getting sick
Money	Gaining weight
National economy	PMS acne
Test in two days	Kids sleeping
Packing for a vacation	Roommate

2. Categorize the worries into those you can realistically do something about and those you cannot. Identifying and letting go of those areas you cannot control is critical. Once an item is in that column, you no longer need to feel pressured to act on it or worry about it right now.

HAVE CONTROL OVER	DO NOT HAVE CONTROL OVER
House is a mess	National economy
Money	Kids getting sick
Test in two days	PMS acne
Packing for vacation	Kids sleeping
Gaining weight	Roommate

3. To put a spin on this exercise, we will now add three columns to the "Have Control Over" category. At first, I only had my clients use the above two columns, but I soon found out that most people who worry tend to take the whole world on their shoulders. They are perfectionists. They would tell me they could or should be able to control nearly everything on their list. The new columns listed below will give a time reference to your worries or prompt you to make lists. Take a look at the example below to see how this works.

Have Control Over			Do NOT Have Control Over
Can Do Right Now	*Need to Set Up Mini Goals For*	*Can Make a List For*	
• House is a mess —clean one area and save the rest for tomorrow	• Money— can take time to make a budget later • Gaining weight —set up exercise & food goal for week	• Test —things to study • Packing —items to take	• National economy • Kids getting sick • PMS acne • Kids sleeping • Roommate

4. After completing this exercise you can see which areas you have to let go of at 10:30 p.m. Then you can feed the dog, do the dishes, and create a simple study list as well as a list of items to pack. Once the lists are made, you could read an inspiring book, take a shower, or do something else relaxing before going to bed. You are in control, you have put things in perspective, and, most importantly, you have stopped the "worry wheel." The key elements to remember are (1) Identify Proper Time Frames, (2) Set Mini Goals, and (3) Create Lists.

1. Identify Proper Time Frames

This may be the moment when you have to retire your Superwoman cape. No one can get everything done right now. Prioritizing worries based on importance and realistic time frames is the key. First, you must learn to realistically prioritize "Have Control Over" worries into the following categories: "Must Do Right Now," "Can Wait Until Tomorrow," "Will Work Toward This Month," and "I Just Can't Do Much About It Right Now." After you do this, you can focus on the short-term worries, allowing for flexibility. I must say I'm the worst at flexibility when it comes to my schedule. In fact, my husband teases me all the time about messing up my own plans. Believe it or not, I can struggle with a surprise vacation because it goofs up my laundry schedule! The ability to temporarily rearrange worries into the "Don't Have Control

Over" category has become very useful for me. Try letting go of some control; you'll be letting go of a lot of worry as well.

2. Set Mini Goals

The next step deals with long-term worries. Mini goals are the best way to set yourself up for success. For example, if one of your consistent worries is to lose weight and you place this worry in the "Have Control Over" category, the worry will not go away until the weight does. When dealing with achievements that may take some time, you must be rational in determining stepping stones to get there.

A starting point may be to exercise three days this week. This worry can then be placed in the "Have Control Over" category as a goal for tomorrow or possibly the day after. The chance to actually *do* something about the worry is in the near future. Success is in sight. After you achieve each stepping stone, your worry of failing will diminish and a habit will begin to take over. Progress towards a goal, no matter how big or small, will be the evidence of your success.

Worries can also escalate with added time pressures. For time-sensitive deadlines, learn to prepare and set up mini goals or deadlines in advance to avoid feeling overwhelmed. My favorite example is the crazy Christmastime mom. I know I've been there—so much to get done, so little time. Everything has to be perfect and the deadline is absolutely critical. I have wasted more than one December worrying about all the tasks

I *had* to do and forgetting to take time for my family. Setting a flexible schedule of reasonable mini goals and time frames for each task in November has saved me. Christmas cards one week, last-minute shopping another, deliver friend gifts the next, etc. A little bit of "gentle planning" can go a long way.

3. Create Lists

Many worries are centered around the notion of forgetting. What if I forget to pack the sunscreen? What if I forget to complete an assignment? What if I forget my child's piano lesson? What if I forget to pay that bill? My "worry wheel" absolutely loves these kind of concerns. Soon I feel like I won't be able to remember anything.

A classic example is packing for a family trip. Men typically do not even think about any of the details until half an hour to an hour before it's time to go. Women, on the other hand, may start to worry about packing weeks in advance. What type of clothes should I take? What will the weather be like? What will my kids need for the car/plane ride? What medication needs to go? I can get stressed out just thinking about an *imaginary* vacation! To-do lists are the simple answer to this problem. Once you've thought about and decided upon items to take, *write them down*. Create categories if you want. Have different papers for each family member or color-code items that different people are in charge of. Either way, you are eliminating the "forget worry." The action of creating lists moves you forward and negates the running-in-place feeling. This sounds very simple but it works. Try it the next time you feel bombarded by details.

The bottom line: Learn to let some things go, become more realistic, and choose action over worry by creating mini goals and lists.

Personal Worry Chart

Have Control Over			Do NOT Have Control Over
Can Do Right Now	Need to Set Up Mini Goals For	Can Make a List For	

CHAPTER 11

Get a Grip on What-If

What if I fail this test? What if I gain weight? What if I don't get the job? What if I can't sleep tonight? What if I overeat again? I'm pretty sure you've had at least one of these thoughts before, maybe even today. Worrying about the future is normal in small degrees. The problem with *what-if*s is that the present can be taken over by all the negative possibilities of the future. You can quickly find yourself wasting your life away with all of the worst-case scenarios of the future. This style of thinking can become quite addictive and can combine with worry and negative thinking to make your life miserable.

First, let's define *what-if* thinking, also known as anticipatory anxiety, and then discuss its connection with worry. In *Attacking Anxiety & Depression,* we read, "Anticipatory anxiety is that anxiety which is experienced with the initial thought and anticipation of doing something" (p. 8-2). This anticipation frequently leads to negative, frightening thoughts of the future. These thoughts can often be powerful enough to start spinning the "worry wheel" we discussed in chapter 10. Your wheel can reach intense speeds when your worries relate to unpredictable events in the future. You can't do anything about the concerns right then, so your mind has time to play around with a scary thought until it becomes a monster. A favorite example I use with my clients, who are typically college students, is the fear of finals week. Those who tend to "*what-if* think" can start feeling anxious about finals several months before they are even scheduled! Two weeks into the semester, when the professor probably hasn't thought twice about the final, a *what-if* thinker might be wrapped up in worries about which questions will be asked on that crucial test. So much wasted time!

A pessimist's best friend can be *what-if* thinking. When combined with negative thought patterns, the future *what-if*s are always terrible, depressing, and overwhelming. I remember times in my life when I was stuck in this thought cycle. Everything about my future was scary and uncertain. I found myself constantly expressing these fears to my husband. (Bad idea—he is an extreme optimist!) I wanted him to validate my fears and feel sorry for me, take me in his arms, and join my pity parry. Instead, he would only point out the positives, predict great outcomes, and do so with a smile on his face. At the time, I thought he was a bit obnoxious, but now I see how much I needed his perspective and logic. His thoughts were accurate and logical, while mine were overexaggerated and often irrational. Eventually, my husband became a great model to pattern my thoughts after, especially when I realized how happy he allowed himself to be by *living in the moment* instead of dreading the future. Lesson learned? Positive thinking equals more happiness.

So, how do we go about changing the habit of *what-if* thinking? The most successful tool is probably the easiest one I teach. It is simply a matter of flipping the sentence or thought to its exact opposite. An example would be: "What if I feel fat in my swimsuit and it ruins my vacation?" Now the counterpart: "What if I don't feel fat and have a wonderful vacation?" See how easy it is. It doesn't involve a lot of deep, creative thinking, and anyone can quickly come up with an opposite. Now looking back at those two statements, let's explore the feelings and thoughts that would come from them. If I were to dwell on the feeling-fat-vacation thought, I would probably begin to spin my negative worry wheel. I could then begin thinking things like, "I will embarrass myself," "Everyone will make fun of me," "I will be afraid to eat anything," "I will have a horrible time in such a beautiful place and feel so angry and depressed," "My friends/husband will get frustrated with me. They would have more fun without me," "Maybe I should cancel my plans so I won't have to worry about any of this." Can you see how a simple negative prediction can become so fearful and can even seem factual?

Now if I quickly replace my negative *what-if* statement with its opposite, I can focus on the fact that I have a wonderful vacation to look forward to. I can focus on all of the events that have nothing to do with a swimsuit. I can explore clothing options that I feel comfortable and cute in. Maybe a cover-up or skirt that is flattering will make me feel very attractive. What if I love my body enough to accept it and have a great time? How do you feel after that little pep talk? I would expect you to feel happy, hopeful, and peaceful. If you're afraid these positive thoughts may be just too hard to come up with, don't give up hope. Just visit Chapter 8: "The Inner Dialogue" again. It takes a little practice, but the positive *what-if* statement is the best place to start with positive comebacks.

Here are several more examples to bring this point home.

What if I fail this class?
What if I don't fail and I do well?

What if I overeat tonight at the restaurant?
What if I don't overeat and I have a great time?

What if I never feel good about my body?
What if I learn to love and accept all of myself?

What if I can't go to sleep?
What if I can?

What if I don't get my house cleaned or assignment done, etc.?
What if I do?

What if I gain weight on my vacation?
What if I don't?

Pretty simple, right? Hopefully, at least one of those ideas hits home for you. I can't stress enough the impact this simple exercise has had on my life and the lives of my clients. This seems to be the tool that can jump-start all others and eventually lead to positive thinking.

What-If Exercise

List the top concerns you often *what-if* about. Next, create a counter statement. *What if* the positive happens?

1.

    Counterpart:

2.

    Counterpart:

3.

    Counterpart:

4.

    Counterpart:

5.

    Counterpart:

Begin practicing this style of thinking whenever you catch yourself creating negative predictions about the future.

Section 3

YOUR BODY IS A GIFT

One of Satan's most powerful methods for taking the influences of the Holy Ghost away from a woman is to create self-hate. As soon as you start to see yourself as not good enough physically, the ball begins to roll. The mind spends so much of its time putting down areas of the body that soon your personal insecurities and flaws are thrown in as well. You constantly face negative thoughts toward yourself until you forget that you are worthy of love, that you have been blessed with so many gifts, and that you are a child of God. Many righteous, obedient young women fall victim to Satan's power in this way. He puts his foot in the door by convincing us that we need to become physically perfect according to the world's standards. In a General Conference address, Elder Jeffrey R. Holland declared:

I plead with you young women to please be more accepting of yourselves, including your body shape and style, with a little less longing to look like someone else. We are all different. Some are tall, and some are short. Some are round, and some are thin. And almost everyone at some time or other wants to be something they are not! But as one adviser to teenage girls said: "You can't live your life worrying that the world is staring at you. When you let people's opinions make you self-conscious you give away your power. . . . The key to feeling [confident] is to always listen to your inner self—[the real *you]" (Julia DeVillers,* Teen People, Sept. *2005, 104). And in the kingdom of God, the real you is "more precious than rubies" (Prov. 3:15).* (Jeffrey R. Holland, "To Young Women," *Ensign,* Nov. 2005, 28)

Satan tries to tells us that the perfect body will bring us more love, more friends, more success, and more contentment. Unfortunately, the opposite usually occurs. We become so wrapped up in ourselves that we forget to love and serve others. We also deal with failure on a daily basis in our efforts to reach this ideal perfection. Soon our self-confidence is gone and the addictive, negative thought pattern has begun.

My goal is to empower women with the tools they need to take their life back. No more belittling and disliking ourselves. We are worthy of self-acceptance, love, and confidence. We can and should enjoy life in the precious temple each of us has been given. Let us fight for happiness and cultivate gratitude for all that we have. Once we stop hating our body, we will be free to live our life to the fullest.

The exercises in this section will help you identify the areas you need to work on and give you the tools to approach the situation or thoughts in a healthier way. Please put your heart into this. Get on your knees in prayer every day and count your blessings.

CHAPTER 12

Body-Image Tests

Whar I first begin working with a client, I ask her to complete the following exercise. It helps me identify patterns, and it helps the client initiate honesty with herself. You can also benefit from this exercise, so please take the time to make your own personal assessments. In each test, you'll be asked how often you think certain thoughts. Many of these thoughts are extremely negative, and it can be very difficult to admit to thinking this way, but it is vital to identify what you are up against. Before you begin, know that you are not alone and that these thoughts and stressful feelings are more common than you might think!

These exercises are based on tests featured in Thomas F. Cash's *The Body Image Workbook: An 8-Step Program for Learning to Like Your Looks.*

Body-Image Thoughts Test

How often do you say the following statements to yourself?
0 = Never 1 = Sometimes 2 = Moderately Often
3 = Often 4 = Almost Always

Negative Thoughts

___ My life is lousy because of how I look.

___ My looks make me a nobody.

___ With my body, nobody is ever going to love me.

___ I wish I were better looking.

___ I MUST lose weight.

___ They think I look fat.

___ I wish I looked like someone else.

___ I hate my body.

___ How I look ruins everything for me.

___ I never look the way I want to.

___ I'm so disappointed in my appearance.

___ I wish I didn't care about how I look.

___ People notice right off what's wrong with my body.

___ They look better than I do.

___ My clothes just don't fit right.

___ I wish others wouldn't look at me.

___ I can't stand my appearance anymore.

Body-Image Thoughts Test

How often do you say the following statements to yourself?
0 = NEVER 1 = SOMETIMES 2 = MODERATELY OFTEN
3 = OFTEN 4 = ALMOST ALWAYS

POSITIVE THOUGHTS

___ Other people think I am beautiful.

___ I think I am beautiful.

___ I am proud of my body.

___ I can accept my body.

___ I like the way I look.

___ I still think I'm attractive even when I'm with people who are more attractive than me.

___ I don't care if people are looking at me.

___ I look healthy.

___ I like the way I look in my bathing suit.

___ These clothes look good on me.

___ My body isn't perfect, but I think it's attractive.

___ I don't need to change the way I look.

___ People will like me for who I am, not the way I look.

___ I can graciously accept compliments.

(*The Body Image Workbook,* 20–25)

Distressing Body-Image Situations Test

How often do these situations cause you stress?

0 = Never   1 = Sometimes   2 = Moderately Often

3 = Often   4 = Almost Always

___ At social gatherings where I know few people

___ When I am the focus of social attention

___ When people see me before I've "fixed myself up"

___ When people see me from certain angles

___ When someone compliments me about my appearance

___ When I am with people who are talking about weight or dieting

___ When I see attractive people on television or in magazines

___ While trying on new clothes

___ When my clothes don't fit just right

___ After a new haircut

___ When I am not wearing any makeup

___ When I look at myself in the mirror

___ When I see myself in a photograph or videotape

___ When I haven't exercised as much as usual

___ When I am exercising

___ After I have eaten a full meal

___ When I get on the scale

___ When I think about how I may look in the future

___ When anticipating sexual relations

___ When my partner sees me undressed

(*The Body Image Workbook*, 20–25)

After completing this assignment, go back and circle the statements marked with a 4. Look for patterns. Are you mostly concerned with what others think? Are your clothes a big problem? Does the number on the scale play a role? Do you ever think anything positive about yourself? Discovering themes will help you target the best solution.

To go along with this exercise, I would like to share a personal story. A few years ago, when my husband served as the Young Men's leader in our ward, he taught a lesson on respecting women and girls. He asked me to talk to these 16- to 18-year-old young men about the impact they can have on a female's self-esteem. I started the lesson by having the young men fill out the thoughts worksheet you just completed. The results were amazing. There were no 4's on the negative thoughts and hardly any 0's on the positive thoughts—completely opposite of the results I had seen at work, where I counsel mostly with women. As I explained to these boys how most girls would fill out this worksheet, they were astounded. They had no idea that we women spend so much time thinking badly about ourselves, or that we have a hard time extending a compliment to ourselves. With all my might, I tried to help these young men understand the important role they can play in the lives of young women. A compliment can go a long way, I told them, and, on the other hand, a careless negative comment could scar a girl for life. I stressed that these young men should build girls up by offering sincere compliments and focusing on their inner traits, not just their outward appearance. Young women desperately need to know they are valued for who they truly are, not just what they look like.

Part of this validation comes from the opposite sex, but I've found the greatest influence on a girl's body image is her mother. Mothers who frequently diet or make negative comments about their own bodies are setting an extremely dangerous example for their daughters. Most of the deep-rooted eating disorders I deal with began with a mother who had the same destructive issues herself. Mothers need to recognize the standard of self-love they set for their daughters simply by the way they look at themselves. Elder Jeffrey R. Holland emphasized this idea when he stated,

> *Every young woman is a child of destiny and every adult woman a powerful force for good. I mention adult women because, sisters, you are our greatest examples and resource for these young women. And if you are obsessing over being a size 2, you won't be very surprised when your daughter or the Mia Maid in your class does the same and makes herself physically ill trying to accomplish it"* (Holland, "To Young Women," 28).

Mothers, please find ways to love your bodies and then show your daughters that you do. Give frequent compliments to your daughters on both their outward appearance and their inner strengths. Prepare them to face the world knowing they are beautiful inside and out.

As I talk to a client about this worksheet, I often share with her my experience speaking to those young men. I ask the client, when it comes to body acceptance, to pattern her thought processes more closely to those of the opposite sex. I ask her to try to spend less time thinking about her body or comparing it to others. Instead, I tell her, she should spend more time thinking about life!

I also ask each of my clients to spend less time around females who might be very triggering. Living with, training with, working with, or even just hanging out with a bunch of girls can become very damaging to your self-worth. Working with a collegiate gymnastic team taught me that pack behavior is very real when it comes to body-image issues. Living with body- or food-obsessed roommates or family members can do the same thing. Constantly exposing yourself to body comparisons or discussions regarding food, dieting, exercise, clothes, fashion, and weight can make overcoming negative body thoughts a daunting task. Therefore, I encourage each of my clients to surround herself as much as possible with women who build a person up based on personality and inner self, who are not obsessed or dissatisfied with their own bodies, and who do not bring up body-image topics on a regular basis.

Often, I tell my college girls that it will get better when they get married and ditch the girls for a guy. No more mirror comparisons when getting ready in the morning, no more discussions about the latest diet or fashion trend, and no more pity parties around a tub of ice cream if someone gets dumped. Once married, you may deal with more mess, more talk about sports or hunting, or even toilet-seat issues, but none of these encourage negative body thoughts. Bottom line: surround yourself with those who enable you to build self-love, and eliminate or confront those who don't.

CHAPTER 13

Eliminating Physical Triggers

Now that we know what we want and deserve, let's create the tools to make it happen. We'll start with the easiest obstacles and work our way to the difficult ones. On the "Distressing Situations" worksheet, we'll first tackle the triggers that are concrete objects, since objects are so much easier to deal with and manipulate than are people or our thoughts. The objects we will identify include:

- Scales
- Mirrors
- Clothes
- Magazines
- TV and movies
- Body checking

Let's go over each one in detail.

Scales

I often tell my clients, "The scale is the devil!" For those who struggle with body image, nothing can be more damaging than weighing themselves over and over again. When was the last time knowing your weight made you feel good? For most of the women I work with, even a "good number" is scary because it leads to thoughts such as, "Can I stay at this new weight? Does my magic number need to be lower now? What if I can't maintain this new weight?" Of course, not everyone struggles with these thoughts, and some women don't battle with the scale, but I believe the majority of us do. I recommend that you avoid having a scale in your home. If you want to know if you've gained or lost weight, notice how your clothes fit. There is absolutely no reason to know your weight on a daily, weekly, or even monthly basis. Your doctor uses your weight as a piece to the puzzle of your overall health. The Department of Motor Vehicles requires it on your driver's license, but most people fib on that question anyway. The point is, if you feel healthy, your clothes are fitting well, and your habits are maintainable, why do you need a number to verify it?

Those of us who regularly used a scale in the past should ask ourselves this simple question when tempted to jump on: "Can I handle what it tells me?" Every client I've met with could not handle the thoughts and emotions the scale conjured up. Most felt emotions such as panic, defeat, hopelessness, and disgust. All because of a number. I've seen far too many people on their way to recovery who hop on the scale just once and digress weeks or even months in their progress. The obsession with food and body perfection heightens when a number is thrown into the pot. All-or-nothing thinking comes at you with a vengeance: "If the number is where I want it, then I am successful, confident, and valued. If the number is high, I am automatically disgusting, a failure, and of no worth." Another frustrating trend I see is the ever-changing ideal. Once a goal weight is met, it is no longer good enough and an even lower weight becomes the goal. In this game, a person always throws perfection further and further out there each time it is achieved. Nothing is ever good enough. So, in case I haven't stressed it enough, my advice is to get *rid of the scale!*

Mirrors

Mirrors are not as easy to dispose of completely, when compared to scales. After all, we do need to see ourselves to do our hair and makeup. The mirrors we will focus on are full-length mirrors, since they tend to cause most of the heartache. How many times a day do you look in the mirror to point out a body part you hate and then spend the next hour or so beating yourself up about it? For example, a woman was getting fed up with her obsession over her body, especially when it came to mirrors, so she decided to conduct an experiment. She counted both the number of times and the length of time she spent looking in a mirror each day. The amount of her life she had wasted worrying about her appearance shocked her, and it fueled her motivation to stop. In the past, she had taken every possible opportunity to look in a mirror and beat herself up. She would even look in the reflection of her car's window each time she got in or out of the vehicle. The final motivation to change came as she walked her daughter home from school one day. They passed by a mirrored building each day on their way home from school, and the woman habitually checked her body each time they passed by. On this particular day, her daughter had completed a tough assignment and was proudly reporting it to her mother. After they passed the mirrored building, the daughter looked at her mother disappointedly and asked her if she even cared, because she obviously wasn't listening. When this woman's obsession to look at her body got in the way of her daughter's happiness, she made the decision to change.

A few tricks can help you diminish mirror time. The first is to take down any of the full-length mirrors you tend to use to critique yourself. If you are worried about your dress being stuck in your nylons, or if you want to make sure your shoes match, simply look down. The negatives of having a full-length mirror in your home can far outweigh the bad. When looking in a full-length mirror, most women scrutinize their belly or backside or hips and then proceed to bombard themselves with negative thoughts. If completely getting rid of a full-length mirror is not possible, try taping a poster board or large piece of paper on the lower part of the mirror so that you can only see your upper body.

The next trick is to place sticky notes, dry-erase-marker messages, or pictures on your mirrors. These messages can include uplifting quotes, personal compliments, reminders of your achievements, or anything else that is positive. The pictures could be of special memories or important people in your life. Your goal is to put all body thoughts into perspective each time you look in the mirror, instead of picking out all of your flaws and dwelling on them.

The third trick is to avoid unnecessary mirror-checking at places like the gym or a department store, as well as when passing by a reflective building or a car window. Mirror watching can become very habitual and result in an increased frequency of negative body thoughts.

On the campus of the university where I work, a large building with reflective windows sits between the library and the business building. Every student on campus makes regular trips past this building. The windows line the main sidewalk, and the majority of students check themselves out as they pass by. Almost every student I've met with has told me that she can't help but look at her body each time she passes the building, and that most of the time, she is left with negative thoughts that last for several minutes, or even several hours. The challenge I extend to each client is to find something new to look at each time she passes that building. Because her previous vision was so narrow, each young woman now notices many new things when she avoids looking in the reflective windows. She might look at the trees, the other buildings, the flowers, the snow, or even other people's shoes. As long as she doesn't look at the reflective windows, she avoids adding an extra weight of self-doubt each day.

Clothes

If you categorize your clothing by "fat clothes," "now clothes," and "someday-I'll-get-back-into clothes," you need an extreme closet makeover. I want you to start appreciating the "now" body and dressing for it. Which colors look best on you? Which styles fit your body type the best? Feel confident about how you look right now. Get rid of the "someday" clothes! I don't care how skinny you are—if you wear a size smaller than your body, you will feel fat all day. If you can't throw the clothes away or give them to a thrift store, at least put them in storage. To look at the "someday" clothes every time you get dressed will only be discouraging and remind you that your body isn't good enough. How about letting yourself be okay right now? If your jeans are constantly too tight, find some that fit. This doesn't mean you are giving up on losing weight if that is a healthy goal for you. It just means you are giving up the negative body-image thoughts along your weight-loss journey. The pressure—the constant reminder to be thinner—only leads to obsession, depression, and, in most cases, failure. It's the daily habits that initiate weight loss, not the constant reminder from tight-fitting jeans. I've also found that clothes can follow the same pattern as the scale. Once they reach a smaller size, some women no longer consider that acceptable, so their perfect size continues to drop. Your goal should be to dress yourself in a way that makes you feel pretty and attractive now. The kinder you are to your body, the more fulfilled your life can be.

Shopping for clothes can also be a monster, so approach it with a positive attitude. If necessary, pace yourself and only shop for short periods. Take a friend who is always good for a laugh. Shop for accessories in between shopping for clothing; earrings seldom come with a lot of emotional baggage. Also, forget the number on the tag—the size. I've purchased many different sizes of pants in a relatively short period of time, during which my body size didn't change. Clearly, the size number is irrelevant. In addition, as with the number on the scale, you do not have a neon sign on your forehead alerting others to your weight or your pant size. No one else notices or cares but you. If the particular piece of clothing looks good on you, the size listed on the tag shouldn't matter. Finally, when it comes to the dreaded beast, swimsuit shopping, I have only one suggestion. Do your best to ward off any negative thoughts, and for those that stick around only allow them access into your life for one day and then let it go. Swimsuit shopping can be somewhat painful, so allow yourself a little time to process the thoughts if necessary and then *get over it!* The next chapter will provide more suggestions for dealing with these thoughts.

Magazines

Ah, the wonderful world of the air-brushed ideal. The images we see on the cover of many popular magazines do nothing but make us feel inferior. The cover model is flawless in every way. Every strand of hair is in place, and her skin is so smooth that she must not have any pores at all. Well, if it sounds or looks too good to be true, it is. My husband owns an advertising agency and I've seen firsthand the manipulation that can take place with a photo. In baseball terms, our first strike is a mystical ideal that does not even exist.

And what about all the personnel it takes to make someone look like that? How many people work on the wardrobe, makeup, hair, lighting, etc.? How much time does it take to maintain that glamorous look and body? How much waxing, hair dying, bronzing, and working out with a personal trainer are involved, and would I personally want to devote that much time to my appearance? Since I only allot 10 to 15 minutes to doing my hair each day, my answer would obviously have to be *no!* Another component is cost. I'm sure the combined costs for this type of treatment and care would match or exceed the cost of my SUV. There are so many more things to spend money on. Strike two, time and cost.

Finally, the cover of almost every women's magazine is filled with empty promises: "Lose ten pounds in three days!" "Miracle food that melts away the pounds!" "Improve your love life overnight in three easy steps!" "Simple exercises to tone your abs, butt, and thighs." And on and on. These words are simply a marketing ploy to get you to purchase the magazine. We want to hear such phrases, because we wish life worked this way. But nothing about a long-term healthy lifestyle is that easy. Many women believe the gimmicks they found in a magazine, telling me, "I can only eat these types of foods together." "All I have to do are these abdominal exercises to lose the weight." "If I just stay away from this certain food, the pounds will disappear." A hopeful woman will then try one of these gimmicks with high expectations. A week later, she feels like a failure again, thinking she didn't try hard enough or that she will never be worthy of achieving the promised results. Her mind is now filled with even more myths, and the components of a healthy lifestyle seem like a puzzle she will never be able to solve. Strike three: empty promises leave us unfulfilled and frustrated.

After the third strike in baseball, a batter is out. The same should happen to these types of magazines. You know the kind I'm talking about—the ones that focus on glamour and tabloid gossip. Even magazines targeting women's health, fitness, and homemaking skills come packed with a lot of body-image baggage. So many young women I meet with have become fearful of eating almost all types of foods, at any time of day and in any combination, because of the numerous supposed "facts" in a fitness or health magazine. Even if an article contains some truth, it is only part of the puzzle and can be overexaggerated to the point of becoming harmful to the body. If these magazines are triggering to you, please stay away from them. If they make you feel anxious about your body and eating—if they make you feel inferior, confused, or overwhelmed—do not buy them, read them, or even look at them.

Remember, everything in life does not magically fall into place or improve just because you wear the latest fashions, look like a movie star, or have the "perfect" body. Ask a woman who appears in tabloid or glamour magazines if her life is perfect. If she is honest, she will probably tell you that her life is actually quite complicated because of this perceived ideal.

Concerning the world's perceptions about beauty, Elder Jeffrey R. Holland stated:

> *In terms of preoccupation with self and a fixation on the physical, this is more than social insanity; it is spiritually destructive, and it accounts for much of the unhappiness women, including young women, face in the modern world. And if adults are preoccupied with appearance—tucking and nipping and implanting and remodeling everything that can be remodeled—those pressures and anxieties will certainly seep through to children. At some point the problem becomes what the Book of Mormon called "vain imaginations" (1 Ne. 12:18). And in secular society both vanity and imagination run wild. One would truly need a great and spacious makeup kit to compete with beauty as portrayed in media all around us. Yet at the end of the day there would still be those "in the attitude of mocking and pointing their fingers" as Lehi saw (see 1 Ne. 8:27 . . .), because however much*

one tries in the world of glamour and fashion, it will never be glamorous enough. (Holland, "To Young Women," 28)

Television & Movies

If magazines are a difficult trigger for you, this area will most likely be as well. The media attacks from many angles. Entertainment news programs are filled with stories with body-image themes. Who wore the best/worst dress, who gained/lost the most weight, and which absolutely gorgeous person has fallen in love with another absolutely gorgeous person. Constantly viewing these types of shows gives the viewer a false sense of reality. According to these shows, in order to fall in love or have a successful life, you need to look beautiful all of the time and have the perfect body. The constant body-critiquing of others will only increase your analysis of your own body. When I speak to a group, I often begin this topic by stating that in a movie, the male characters are largely overshadowed. Not only do guys spend most of the time looking at the beautiful girl, but women spend almost the entire movie comparing themselves to the beautiful actress. The good-looking male actor just doesn't get much attention. Nearly every girl in the group smiles, while nodding that she too is a victim to body-comparing.

Another drawback from movies and televisions is the character that becomes associated with the body. If the *character* is someone we admire or emulate, we internalize the theory that if we can look like her we might even become like her. Several of my clients wanted to look like Jennifer Aniston, and they actually would obsess about it. Her characters are usually funny, quirky, full of life, and—of course—beautiful. So a woman might think that if she could have a body and face like Jennifer's, all of life's hardships would disappear and her life would turn into a fairy tale. This sounds unrealistic to most people, but when a large percentage of the day is devoted to comparing oneself to a certain person, the fairy tale no longer seems absurd.

A few weeks ago I challenged one of my clients to a star test. I asked her to divide a piece of paper in half. On one half of the piece of paper, she listed all of the negatives to looking just like her favorite female star, and on the other half, she listed all of the benefits. By filling out the negatives first she was able to see this person's life in a more realistic view. Negatives included: no privacy, constant critiquing of appearance; a great deal of time spent on hair, skin, nails, waxing, exercise, etc.; and constant hounding from the paparazzi. After this list was completed the benefits no longer had as much dazzle. If you are fighting your own comparison battle, you might want to look at the whole picture. No one's life is perfect based on appearance. In fact, those who are paid to look perfect often face very difficult obstacles.

Body-Checking

I'm not sure if Webster has an entry for body-checking, but most women know exactly what it means. My own definition states: body checking is the touching, pinching, rubbing, or manipulation of clothing on areas of the body you are dissatisfied with. Constantly sucking in your stomach, tugging at your jeans, touching your thighs, playing with the skin on your underarm, or pinching the area under your chin all qualify as body-checking. If you are unaware of this practice, you may find these descriptions surprising or even humorous. For those addicted to this practice, body checking is a constant reminder of failure or inadequacy. While reading a book, taking a test, or watching TV, an individual can repeatedly check her body in an effort to remind her how fat, unattractive, or lazy she is. Body checkers claim they do this to keep themselves in line with dieting or weight-loss practices. They think constant reminders should keep them on track. Another perceived benefit relates to worry of any kind. A worrier has the notion that if a problem is analyzed and thought about enough, it will magically correct itself. Thus, I believe that deep down, body checkers think that if they frequently assess themselves, the desired body they want will somehow appear. Unfortunately, reminding oneself or thinking about unsatisfactory body parts does not help in achieving the perfect body. In fact, body checking can lead to terrible inner dialogue battles, harsher food/exercise rules, and even more chances to fail. Body checking does not work, and it can only make your life miserable.

That said, body checking is a tough habit to break, because the checking becomes almost like a nervous twitch that a person does unconsciously. Overcoming this pattern takes self-awareness and willpower. To help a client stop body checking, I will encourage her to touch a random body part such as an elbow after each body check, or wash her hands or do any other mundane task she can think of. This process promotes awareness and becomes annoying, so it can help break the habit. If you are a body checker and want to try this process, be patient. Over time, you will see improvements, and the benefits of not checking will motivate you to stop.

We cannot find balance and happiness with ourselves until we have a positive inner dialogue. Body checking, abuse of scales and mirrors, and believing everything we hear or see in the media about beauty, will never let us find happiness. Please ask yourself if it is really worth it before you participate in any of these activities.

CHAPTER 14

ABC Exercise

This exercise identifies the impact that outward triggers can have on your emotions and your overall happiness. It is adapted from Thomas Cash's exercise titled "What Do You See When You Look in the Mirror?" If body image is a very sensitive area for you, start each of these exercises with an anthropologist approach (discussed in the Chapter 4: "Silencing the Food Police"). All you need to do is collect facts. The actions can come later on, after you have acquired more tools. Now let's break down the components of this exercise, look at an example, and discuss ways to make it work for you.

A = Activators

These are specific events and situations that may trigger negative thoughts and feelings about your body.

B = Beliefs

These include the thoughts, perceptions, and interpretations that occur in your mind.

C = Consequences

These are emotional and behavioral reactions that can be broken down even more using a TIDE acronym.

T: Types of emotions—depression, anxiety, anger, etc.

I: Intensity—on a scale from 0 to 10.

D: Duration—how long did the consequences/feelings last?

E: Effects—what did you do? Withdraw, skip a meal, take feelings out on others, etc.

(*The Body Image Workbook,* 57)

Example

A—Watching a popular movie

B—I want to be like the main character— "flirty and thriving." I hate how fat I am. If I was skinny I would have an exciting life. I don't want anyone to see me like this!

C—Consequences

    T—depressed, angry, disappointed

    I—7

    D—1 day

    E—only ate half a bowl of soup and refused to eat dessert at a party. Started counting calories again.

On paper, these feelings and beliefs may seem overexaggerated, harsh, silly, or shallow. Unfortunately, for many people, they are very real and occur much too often. It is amazing how much comparing, assuming, and critiquing goes on in a woman's mind when it comes to appearance.

The purpose of this exercise is to create awareness. By breaking down the consequences and putting the beliefs on paper, a person can assess the sometimes exaggerated effects of such a minor event or action. A simple assumption can ruin an entire day or start the dieting roller coaster all over again. Likewise, in a matter of minutes, media exposure in almost any form can lead to depression and self-hate that can last for hours or even days. When you complete this exercise, you can easily see the exaggerated and worst-case-scenario nature of some of your beliefs. For example, you might think that everything about your life is terrible, that no one will ever like you, or that your body is the cause of anything bad in your life. *Nearly all of our negative beliefs about our bodies are false assumptions.*

Another important component of the exercise is the TIDE answers—the type of emotion, intensity, duration, and effects of an action. The longevity of impact is most eye-opening. A simple assumption that was probably unjustified can ruin an entire night, a quick peek on a scale can bring back feelings of failure that last for weeks, and eating a "forbidden food" can lead to skipping meals for the rest of the day. Identifying the cause-and-effect nature of body-image activators and end results can be an enormous motivator for change. Many of my clients state that they are ready to stop participating in a triggering action simply because they are tired of dealing with such a harsh result.

Lessons Learned from A & C Components

- Look for trigger trends—Do you compare all day long?
  Are most of your triggers media based?
- Categorize intensity—Which areas cause the largest
  reaction? You may want to address those first.
- Analyze the range of your reactions—Do you typically
  lash out, keep it all in, or even participate in self-
  destructive dieting behaviors? Do you need to have more
  relaxing, positive distractions? Do you need someone
  to talk to? Do you need professional help with eating
  habits?

ABC Body-Image Worksheet

A = Activator:

B = Beliefs:

C = Consequences

      T = Types of emotions:

      I = Intensity (0—10):

      D = Duration:

      E = Effects:

CHAPTER 15

A-thru-E Help Sheet

This chapter builds on everything we learned in chapter 14. We are simply adding D and E components to the equation. The D is "Disputing by Corrective Thinking," and the E is "Effects of Corrective Thinking." We will discuss the components, look at examples, and then outline ideas to put the components into action.

Chapter 8, "The Inner Dialogue," is strongly correlated with this chapter and may be a good reference.

Full Model

A = Activators

B = Beliefs

C = Consequences

D = Disputing by Corrective Thinking

E = Effects of Corrective Thinking

(*The Body Image Workbook*, 140)

The A, B, and C themes are the same as in chapter 14. Let's talk about D and E.

Disputing with Positive Thoughts

"Disputing with Positive Thoughts," letter D, consists of turning a negative, self-damaging thought completely around. For example, if you were to say, "I am so ugly," a possible dispute would be, "I am so beautiful." The actual process of re-scripting a thought this way is quite simple. The problem most women face is buying into or believing the positive counter statement. In fact, many women won't take the time or effort to even create such a thought, because thinking positively about themselves seems so foreign. It is easier to continue beating themselves up and following the negative path of least resistance. But I promise that this cognitive restructuring is your best weapon in fighting the body-image battle and finding peace. The key is to practice, practice, practice. In fact, research has shown that whether a person actually believes the new positive thought or not appears to be irrelevant in producing behavioral changes (see Marcia Herrin, *Nutrition Counseling in the Treatment of Eating Disorders* [New York: Brunner-Routledge, 2003], 30).

The bottom line is—no matter how cheesy, silly, or unbelievable the positive thought may be, it is actually the pivotal tool in getting better. More than anything, you just need to become better at positive thinking. Your brain is not used to going to that happy place, and doing so may feel painful or awkward at first. With consistent practice of positive thinking, the fog will begin to lift and you will be able to see your whole self again and embrace all that is good in you. For help in getting used to turning your body-image thoughts around, refer to the "positive comeback" section of the chart on page 134.

Effects of Corrective Thinking

Letter E, "Effects of Corrective Thinking," refers to the incentives or payoffs for persevering through this behavior-changing process. I want you to identify and write down the emotional, mental, social, and even spiritual effects of thinking more positively about your body. Do you have more mental power to devote to a hard school or work project? Do you have more time to enjoy the things you love to do? Are you a better wife/mother/daughter/friend? Are you able to feel closer to your Father in Heaven? If you are putting forth the necessary effort, after a few weeks you should be able to answer *yes* to all of these questions. Positive results fuel desire. Set aside some time to yourself to evaluate the benefits you receive from this exercise. They will be the motivation you need to overcome the body image obstacles life throws at you.

Examples:

A: Eating "forbidden" foods.

B: I am fatter just thinking about the food. I can't be thin if I eat that. If I like it, I won't be able to stop.

C: Frustrated, anxious, overwhelmed.

D: I must eat to live. Food is fuel. I deserve to eat and be healthy. I have the tools to stop eating.

E: Able to choose the food I really wanted. Enjoyed eating and then quickly moved on to an enjoyable activity.

A: Being around thin people.

B: I am a failure. I'm a giant. What is my problem? I have no self-control. I could try harder.

C: Jealous, self-hatred, sad

D: I am a unique individual. Comparing my negative qualities to others positive qualities is unfair.

E: Able to socialize at the party. Found others liked me for my personality. Realized just because a person is thin, does not mean they have it all. (Some were actually boring.)

Here are some examples of negative thoughts and the positive comebacks you might employ.

NEGATIVE THOUGHT	POSITIVE COMEBACK
• I hate my body. • My stomach is disgusting. • Everyone notices all of my acne. • My hair is terrible today. • No one will like me at this weight. • I am so uncoordinated • I am so fat.	• I love who I am. • My favorite body part is my feet. • No one has time to study me that close. • I look good in this color. • My friends love the inner me. • I can sing really well • I am alive and have this great body

𝒜-thru-ℰ Body-Image Makeover Exercise

A = Activator:

B = Beliefs:

C = Consequences
      T = Types of emotions:

      I = Intensity (0—10):

      D = Duration:

      E = Effects:

D = Disputing by Corrective Thinking:

E = Effects of Corrective Thinking:

CHAPTER 16

Destructive Thinking Styles

The following are styles of thinking used by those who suffer from a negative body image. Each style of thinking is followed by a new inner voice. Use these thoughts and questions to identify how you can become kinder to yourself. At the end of this chapter is a worksheet where you can write down your thoughts, action plans, and helpful dialogue phrases.

Dichotomous Thinking (Black or White)

Everything is seen in extremes. I'm either perfect or I'm a failure. I'm either weigh XXX or I'm fat. New Inner Voice:

- I can see shades of gray.
- Not being a "10" doesn't make me a "1."
- Imperfections make me unique.
- Do I judge everyone else by these extremes?
- Whom am I trying to impress or please?

Unrealistic Ideals

Comparing self against the media. New Inner Voice:
- If the ideal body were everything, then only good-looking people would have a happy, successful life.
- I don't have to have a perfect body to be attractive or confident.
- No one's body is perfect. Even models have imperfections that are PhotoShop'd.

Unfair comparisons—comparing your weaknesses to others strengths. New Inner Voice:
- I need to start comparing fair. What are some of my strengths?
- What trivial things can I compare? (belts, shoes, watches, etc.)

Unrealistic Ideals: Comparing Fair Exercise

If you are constantly comparing yourself to others who have everything you don't, STOP! Start taking the whole package into perspective. If you have straight hair, maybe you constantly compare yourself to women who have beautiful curls—you feel jealous of or inferior to these women. Have you ever thought that the chick with bouncing curls might hate her thighs and constantly compare herself to everyone who has thin legs? No one has it all. Stop assuming that the life of the girl who supposedly has everything you want is perfect. You never know what challenges and insecurities she faces. Also, every time you compare and lose, force yourself to compare and WIN! What do you have that the girl you just compared to doesn't? Are your eyes prettier? Do you have a better complexion? This will be hard at first and you may feel you are being arrogant to think this way. Don't worry; if you are reading this book, I doubt vanity is your thing. It may feel wrong or bad to put yourself above someone else, but isn't it equally as wrong to put yourself down on a regular basis? You must realize that you have wonderful qualities too.

Linda to write text

Negative Filter

Focusing on a negative feature and disqualifying anything positive. New Inner Voice:

- Why not accentuate my positives?
- What are my three favorite body parts?
- What do others compliment me about?
- Is obsessing about my abs, arms, backside, etc., getting me anywhere?
- Avoid name-calling and derogatory descriptions such as "Blubber Butt."

Assuming the Worst

Assuming others think the same negative things you do. New Inner Voice:

- What has actually been said?

- What are the facts?
- Don't waste time on the unknown.
- Who cares what others think?

I Have to Be Beautiful to Be Loved

Believing that acceptance and love are based solely on outward appearance. New Inner Voice:

- My actions prove who I really am.
- Do I still love others when they look imperfect?
- Changing the way I look will not make me more loved. Changing the way I act will.
- Real love is more than skin deep.

Predicting a Terrible Future

Believing that you must look perfect in order to succeed and be happy. Examples: "I'm too ugly or fat to ever get married." "I'm not pretty enough to get a good job." New Inner Voice:

- What if I am pretty enough to get married?
- What if my future husband thinks I'm hot?
- What if my knowledge and skills are enough to get myself a great job?
- Use the *what-if* strategies in chapter 11.

"I Just Can't"

Restricting actions and activities because of your body. Example: "I can't go to the beach or aerobics looking like this." New Inner Voice:

- Who says I can't?
- What action plan do I need to create so I feel more comfortable?
- What would make it easier? (Buy a cute cover-up for the beach, go to aerobics with friends, etc.)

Overcoming Destructive Thinking Styles

List your top-three destructive thinking styles, create new inner voice messages, and address an action plan if necessary.

DESTRUCTIVE THINKING STYLE:
New Inner Voice:

Action Plan:

DESTRUCTIVE THINKING STYLE:
New Inner Voice:

Action Plan:

DESTRUCTIVE THINKING STYLE:
New Inner Voice:

Action Plan:

CHAPTER 17

Pampering Activities

Taking care of yourself is vital in dealing with emotional eating, and in the case of negative body image it is just as important. You will never be able to accept your body if you cannot do nice things for it. Often these "pampering activities" enhance your overall mood and give you an optimistic outlook, and they may even increase your outer beauty. I encourage my clients to do at least one pampering activity every day. Remember that these activities do not need to be expensive or time consuming. My personal favorite is a long, relaxing bath after my kids have gone to bed. I love to lock myself in the bathroom with a good book and escape from the world for a while. If you never find an outlet for your frustrations and negativity, your destructive body-image thoughts will remain with you all day. *Find a way to escape from your thoughts.* Hopefully, the following list will give you some ideas. Please invest the time to do something nice for yourself and your body. The rewards will be immeasurable.

ACTIVE	RELAXING
• Take a walk	• Shower
• Play a team sport	• Bubble bath
• Water sports	• Manicure
• Hiking or rock climbing	• Pedicure
• Golf	• Body massage
• Tennis or racquetball	• Back rub
• Skiing	• Facial
• Playing pool or Ping-Pong	• Scalp massage
• Dancing	• Lotioning your body
• Bowling	
• Gardening or yard work	
• Lifting weights	
• Aerobics	
• Yoga or Pilates	
• Roller-blading or ice-skating	
• Swimming	
• Running or jogging	
• Ballet	
• Martial rts	
• Bike riding	
• Horseback riding	

AESTHETICALLY FUN	MIND
• Cosmetic makeover • Wearing favorite jewelry • Wearing perfume • Coloring or cutting your hair	• Read a favorite book • Cooking • Board games • Jigsaw puzzles • Journal writing • Crossword puzzles • Sudoku • Computer games • E-mailing or letter writing
ENTERTAINING	SPIRITUAL
• Plays • Concerts • Playing games with friends	• Reading scriptures or other religious books • Journal writing • Reading your journal • Prayer or meditation

**When participating in physical activities, remember to focus only on benefits that DO NOT relate to burning calories or sculpting the body; for example, better mood, increased energy, social interaction, etc.

Homework (a Favorite!)

Pamper yourself at least once each day, remembering that it doesn't have to take a lot of time or money. Be creative and, most importantly, enjoy yourself.

CHAPTER EIGHTEEN

Body Gratitude

Essentially, gratitude is the answer to any body-image problem. If you are truly grateful for everything your body is and allows you to do, you will not be able to despise it. In the words of Harold A. Frost:

> *I marvel at the miracle of the human mind and body. Have you ever contemplated the wonders of yourself, the eyes with which you see, the ears with which you hear, the voice with which you speak? No camera ever built can compare with the human eye. No method of communication ever devised can compare with the voice and the ear. No pump ever built will run as long or as efficiently as the human heart. No computer or other creation of science can equal the human brain. What a remarkable thing you are. You can think by day and dream by night. You can speak and hear and smell. Look at your finger. The most skillful attempt to reproduce it mechanically has resulted in only a crude approximation. The next time you use your finger, watch it, look*

at it, and sense the wonder of it. (Harold A. Frost, "The Thinness Obsession," *Ensign,* Jan. 1990, 71)

My clients are used to me using the term "pity party" when discussing body-image experiences. Feeling sorry for yourself or blaming all of life's problems on an imperfect body are the main guests in this pity party. Gone are any grateful thoughts regarding health, sight, mobility, etc. Nothing in life matters because your stomach is chubby, your thighs are huge, or your arms are flabby. Positive inner qualities, personal relationships, and exciting life events are not allowed to enter the picture because your body is imperfect and therefore you feel you are worthless and a failure. While these statements may sound harsh and unbelievable, they are very real and often mild in comparison to the actual dialogue going on during an intense "pity party." While these exaggerated thoughts may not be what you truly believe, when 90 to 95% of your thoughts each day are targeted around hating your body, they become very real and very frightening.

So, how do you stop feeling sorry for yourself and letting these thoughts consume your life? You constantly remind yourself of everything you are grateful for. You count your blessings. What does your body allow you to do and experience? What physical blessings and opportunities do you have that others do not? What is beautiful about your body? What are your favorite body parts? I would guess that many of you reading this book may not have explored the answers to these questions in a very long time. In order for you to love yourself completely, you must learn how to thinking positively and be genuinely grateful for your entire body!

Start a Gratitude Journal

A gratitude journal can help you cultivate appreciation for your own body. Tips for starting a gratitude journal include:

- Keep the journal by your bed. Each night, write down two things your body let you do that day.
- Record compliments in your gratitude journal. The compliments should come both from those around you and from yourself.
- List your favorite three parts of your body.
- Record at least three accomplishments in your journal each day, noting whether your appearance had anything to do with the accomplishment.
- Think about what you have that others may not—health, family, home, sight, hearing, etc.
- Make a list of your talents and positive qualities.

When life is put into perspective, how we actually look does not mean that much. A simple experience from my own life illustrates this. A few years ago, I decided to dye my hair a darker color to achieve a new "fall look." Although my husband said it didn't look that bad, I absolutely hated it. I cried for hours, wore a hat or put my hair up in a ponytail, and avoided any social events for the first few days. My "pity party" had convinced me that my life was over because I looked so terrible. Then I received some beautiful insight. I realized my adorable little boy didn't even notice that anything had changed. He looked at me with those same sparkling blue eyes and continued to give me the all-encompassing smile he saved just for Mom. He loved me no matter what, and he needed me no matter how I looked. *Who I was* mattered to him, not what I looked like. The impact this made on how I view myself was priceless. My worth comes from within! Instead of focusing on what I didn't have (perfectly colored hair), I learned that I needed to focus on what I did have (a sweet little boy, the chance to be a mother, and the opportunity to stay at home and raise my son).

Never forget that you are special, that there are people around you who love you and need you. Your abilities, knowledge, and personality are what really matter. Acknowledge the precious gift of womanhood and all that it entails. President James E. Faust's comments on femininity give us added insight:

> *I wonder if you sisters fully understand the greatness of your gifts and talents and how all of you can achieve the "highest place of honor" in the Church and in the world. One of your unique, precious, and sublime gifts is your femininity, with its natural grace, goodness, and divinity. Femininity is not just lipstick, stylish hairdos, and trendy clothes. It is the divine adornment of humanity. It finds expression in your qualities of your capacity*

to love, your spirituality, delicacy, radiance, sensitivity, creativity, charm, graciousness, gentleness, dignity, and quiet strength. It is manifest differently in each girl or woman, but each of you possesses it. Femininity is part of your inner beauty. (James E. Faust, "Womanhood: The Highest Place of Honor," *Ensign,* May 2000, 95)

Every spirit child of our Father in Heaven is special, unique, and beautiful in his or her own way. Embrace your beauty!

APPENDIX

Scriptural Treasures

Body and Spirit

"Know ye not that ye are the temple of God, and that the Spirit of God dwelleth in you?" (1 Cor. 3:16).

". . . in the image of God made he man . . ." (Gen. 9:6).

"I will make a man more precious than fine gold" (Isa. 13:12).

"Remember the worth of souls is great in the sight of God" (D&C 18:10).

"Whereby are given unto us exceeding great and precious promises; that by these ye might be partakers of the divine nature . . ." (2 Pet. 1:4).

"The Lord seeth not as man seeth; for man looketh on the outward appearance, but the Lord looketh on the heart" (1 Sam. 16:7).

"And charity suffereth long and is kind, and envieth not, and is not puffed up, seeketh not her own . . . " (Moroni 7:45).

Food

"Yea, all things which come of the earth, in the season thereof, are made for the benefit and the use of man, both to please the eye and to gladden the heart;

Yea, for food and for raiment, for taste and for smell, to strengthen the body and to enliven the soul.

And it pleaseth God that he hath given all these things unto man; for unto this end were they made to be used, with judgment, not to excess, neither by extortion" (D&C 59:18–20).

"And every man that striveth for the mastery is temperate in all things" (1 Cor. 9:25).

Anxiety

"Therefore, let the morrow take thought for the things of itself" (D&C 84:84). (*What-if* thinking)

"The Lord will give strength unto this people, the Lord will bless His people with peace" (Psalms 29:11).

"For God is not the author of confusion, but of peace" (1 Cor. 14:33).

"The Lord lift up his countenance upon thee and give thee peace" (Num. 6:26).

"These things I have spoken unto you, that in me ye might have peace. In the world ye shall have tribulation: but be of good cheer; I have overcome the world" (John 16:33).

"Trust in the Lord with all thine heart; and lean not unto thine own understanding. In all thy ways acknowledge him, and he shall direct thy paths" (Proverbs 3:5–6).

Gratitude

"And let the peace of God rule in your hearts . . . and be ye thankful" (Col. 3:15).

"Thou shalt thank the Lord thy God in all things" (D&C 59:7).

"In every thing give thanks: for this is the will of God in Christ Jesus concerning you" (1 Thes. 5:18).

ABOUT THE AUTHOR

Brooke Parker, a registered dietitian, holds a degree in nutrition from Utah State University. Currently, Brooke serves as the dietitian for the entire student body at the university, where she has worked with eating-disordered clients for several years. She is passionate about helping women overcome eating disorders and body-image issues. Physicians and therapists frequently refer their eating-disordered patients and clients to her.

Brooke and her husband live in northern Utah with their three young children. She loves being a mother and all that comes with it. She also enjoys gardening, family vacations, reading, golfing, and snow skiing.

Index